DAVID WALKER'S APPEAL
TO THE
COLOURED CITIZENS
OF THE WORLD

DAVID WALKER'S
APPEAL
TO THE
COLOURED CITIZENS
OF THE WORLD

Edited and with a
New Introduction and Annotations
by
Peter P. Hinks

The Pennsylvania State University Press
University Park, Pennsylvania

Library of Congress Cataloging-in-Publication Data

Walker, David, 1785–1830.
   [Walker's appeal, in four articles]
   David Walker's appeal to the coloured citizens of the world /
edited and with an introduction by Peter P. Hinks.
      p.   cm.
   Originally published as: Walker's appeal, in four articles.
Boston : D. Walker, 1829.
   Includes bibliographical references and index.
   ISBN 0-271-01993-X (cloth : alk. paper)
   ISBN 0-271-01994-8 (pbk.: alk. paper)
   1. Slavery—United States.   2. Slaves—United States—Social
conditions.   I. Hinks, Peter P.   II. Title.
E446.W177 2000
305.896′073—dc21   99-046749

Sixth printing 2012

It is the policy of The Pennsylvania State University Press to use
acid-free paper for the first printing of all clothbound books.
Publications on uncoated stock satisfy the minimum requirements
of American National Standard for Information Sciences—
Permanence of Paper for Printed Library Materials, ANSI
Z39.48–1992.

To Aoife Eileen

CONTENTS

ACKNOWLEDGMENTS

I would like to thank all of the following individuals for their careful and thoughtful readings of the Introduction and other components of this edited volume: James Brewer Stewart, Leon Jackson, Douglas Egerton, Patrick Rael, and Jack McKivigan. As always, Peter Potter, my editor at Penn State Press, has been patient, insightful, and warmly supportive.

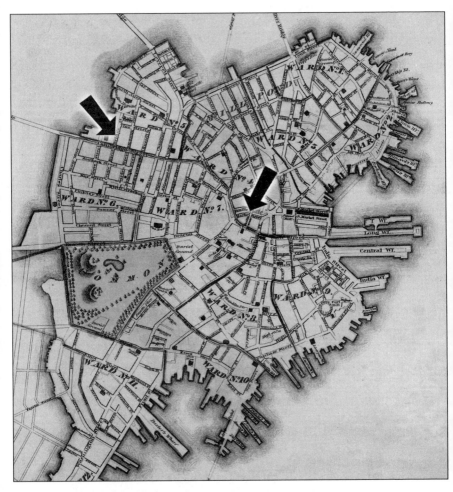

David Walker's Boston. The arrow on the left points to Bridge Street, where Walker owned a house in the late 1820s. (The Massachusetts General Hospital complex stands there today.) The right arrow points to Brattle Street, site of Walker's used clothing shop (on the edge of the current Faneuil Hall Marketplace). (From William B. Annin and George G. Smith, *Plan of Boston* [detail]. Courtesy, Harvard Map Collection.)

INTRODUCTION

"The most noble, fearless, and undaunted David Walker"

One day in Boston in the late 1820s, David Walker was walking on the city's famed Beacon Hill, the top of which was crowned with the Massachusetts State House—one of the nation's most prized symbols of its victorious fight for independence from foreign control, for representative democracy, and for an enlightened, responsible, and free citizenry. Boston had always seemed to hold such meaning and import to America, even at its very origin, when one of its founding fathers, John Winthrop, heralded its birth with a pronouncement that was both encomium and caveat: "We shall be like a City upon a hill; the eyes of all people are on us."[1] David Walker, although black, poor, and deemed incapable by white society of contributing to this mission, embraced Winthrop's convictions, and his *Appeal to the Coloured Citizens of the World* would hold Boston—and America—to these noble and stringent ideals.

While the State House seemed to embody mission, virtue, and accessibility, the very hill on which it stood actually contained a very complex and highly stratified world. Immediately east of the capitol building ran Beacon, Chesnut, and Sumner Streets on which reared the city's grandest homes, belonging to Boston's most powerful families. To them, their proximity to the State House reinforced their intimate and historical bond with it.

---

1. John Winthrop, "A Model of Christian Charity," in Perry Miller, ed., *The American Puritans: Their Prose and Poetry* (New York: Columbia University Press, 1956), 83.

But due north and directly behind the building lay a very different world. Such streets as Belknap, Southack, and Russell held a significant number of the city's working class. Although this neighborhood was predominantly white, it also had the largest concentration of Boston's African Americans, more than 50 percent of them or about 1,000 inhabitants by the late 1820s. They were overwhelmingly poor, uneducated, confined to the most menial occupations, and completely unrepresented at the State House. They were tolerated in the State House only as servants to whites, otherwise only venturing by it as many of them surmounted Belknap on their short way to Chestnut, where they washed dishes, cooked meals, blacked boots, chopped wood, and performed countless other necessary but ordinary tasks for the city's elite. Their proximity to the State House served only to highlight their exclusion from it and from the polity it embodied. These two worlds, while closely related in space, were also wholly distinct and unequal.[2]

Perhaps this day David Walker passed the State House and was stung once again by being so close to this paradoxical exemplar. He may also have noticed in a shop or tavern window one of the innumerable cartoons regularly displayed in the city which ridiculed African American physiognomy and culture in the most humiliating and vulgar manner.[3]

2. Regarding social stratification and racial inequality in early antebellum Boston, see, for example, James and Lois Horton, *Black Bostonians: Family Life and Community Struggle in the Antebellum North* (New York: Holmes & Meier Publishers, 1979), and Peter Hinks, *To Awaken My Afflicted Brethren: David Walker and the Problem of Antebellum Slave Resistance* (University Park: The Pennsylvania State University Press, 1997), 63–90.

3. Hosea Easton, a black contemporary of David Walker's who also lived in Boston in the late 1820s, remarked in a treatise that "cuts and placards descriptive of the Negroe's deformity, are every where displayed. . . . Many of the popular book stores, in commercial towns and cities, have their show-windows lined with them. The bar-rooms of the most popular public houses in the country, sometimes have their ceiling literally covered with them. This display of American civility is under the daily observation of every class of society, even in New England." "A Treatise on the Intellectual Character, and the Civil and Political Condition of the Colored People of the U. States; and the Prejudice Exercised towards Them," in George R. Price and James Brewer Stewart, eds., *To Heal the Scourge of Prejudice: The Life and Writings of Hosea Easton* (Amherst: University of Massachusetts Press, 1999), 106–7.

Perhaps he also encountered some white male "toughs" who occupied the hill and made daily sport of insulting African Americans by hurling racial and sexual epithets and assaulting them physically.[4] Everywhere he looked were the signs and incidents of white Boston's disdain for the dignity and rights of African Americans. "Even here in Boston, pride and prejudice have got to such a pitch!" Walker raged in his *Appeal*.[5]

As he descended the north slope of Beacon Hill and entered the heart of black Boston, Walker met an acquaintance with a large string of boots to black over his shoulder.[6] Smoldering from the routine indignities he had just endured, Walker hailed him and exclaimed: "What a miserable set of people we are. We are so subjected under the whites." Then, condemning their confinement to the lowliest and most servile occupations, Walker looked to his colleague for commiseration. Instead he was confronted with his guileless assertion "I am completely happy!!! I never want to live any better or happier than when I can get a plenty of boots and shoes to clean!!!" Startled and infuriated, Walker could only

---

For an example of such racist iconography and corresponding dialect, see Horton, *Black Bostonians*, illustration between pp. 80 and 81. For examples of such cartoons in Philadelphia at the same time, and for an accompanying analysis, see Gary Nash, *Forging Freedom: The Formation of Philadelphia's Black Community, 1720–1840* (Cambridge: Harvard University Press, 1988), 253–59.

4. Prince Hall, a leader of black Boston at the turn of the century and the founder of the African Masonic movement, recounted how African Americans must "bear up under the daily insults we meet with in the streets of Boston, much more on public days of recreation. How at such times are we shamefully abused, and that to such a degree, that we may truly be said to carry our lives in our hands, and the arrows of death are flying about our heads. Helpless women have their clothes torn from their backs . . . [and] twenty or thirty cowards have fallen upon one man." Prince Hall, "[Extract from] A Charge Delivered to the African Lodge, June 24, 1797, at Menotomy, Massachusetts," in Benjamin Brawley, *Early American Negro Writers* (Chapel Hill: University of North Carolina Press, 1935), 98–99. These types of attacks were routine well into the nineteenth century.

5. *David Walker's Appeal to the Coloured Citizens of the World*, ed. Peter P. Hinks (University Park: The Pennsylvania State University Press, 2000), 42. (Hereafter cited as *Appeal*.)

6. *Appeal*, 31–32.

throw up his hands and retort: "Oh! how can those who are actuated by avarice only, but think, that our Creator made us to be an inheritance to them for ever, when they see that our greatest glory is centered in such mean and low objects?" His anger was directed at, as he put it, "being *happy* in such low employments," at the man's acquiescence to the near total curtailment of opportunity for African Americans, not with the job itself or the man's commitment to labor. Apparently blind to, or simply accepting of, his confinement and subjection, the bootblack was for Walker a paradigm of what needed to be changed about the level of understanding and aspirations of the mass of African Americans.

David Walker's *Appeal to the Coloured Citizens of the World*— one of the nineteenth century's most incisive and vivid indictments of American racism and the insidious undermining it wrought on the black psyche—spoke directly to the bootblack and to the hundreds of thousands of similarly narrowed African Americans. Through the pamphlet, Walker intended nothing less than "to awaken his slumbering and afflicted brethren" to the fabric of false and dangerous illusions about their conditions and character woven into their consciousness by centuries of oppression, and to summon them to strength and entitlement.[7] David Walker would have agreed with the baleful pronouncement of Richard Allen, founder of the African Methodist Episcopal (AME) church and a man he revered, who wrote: "The vile habits often acquired in a state of servitude are not easily thrown off."[8] The *Appeal* was meant to throw its shoulder full force into that endeavor.

"I am one of the oppressed, degraded and wretched sons of Africa": The Life and Times of David Walker

Few knew the world of black America as thoroughly as David Walker did. He may well have traveled the length and

---

7. *Appeal*, 5.
8. Richard Allen, "An Address To Those Who Keep Slaves and Approve

breadth of the new nation and been exposed to its racial horrors in various settings, North and South. Probably in or about 1796, Walker was born free in Wilmington, North Carolina, apparently to a free black woman and a male slave. No records of his birth or of his parents remain. Nothing is known with certainty of his years in Wilmington, but the town and the entire region along the lower Cape Fear River in the southeastern corner of the state were filled with both slavery at its most brutal and African Americans at their most resourceful and independent. By 1800, two-thirds, or 1,134, of Wilmington's inhabitants were black, and of these all but nineteen were slaves. Slaves performed most of the labor—skilled and unskilled—that made the region the nation's leading producer of naval stores and a significant supplier of lumber and rice. Slaves in Wilmington were famous throughout coastal North Carolina as building designers, carpenters, masons, plasterers, and sometimes—in the case of free blacks with slave crews—even as contractors. They were also celebrated as excellent rivermen who mastered the deceptive currents and obstacles of the region's most important thoroughfares—its rivers—to bring goods to the port of Wilmington.[9]

After their labors, the slaves of Wilmington nourished their souls at the Methodist church they had established in Wilmington. It is likely that the foundation of Walker's lifelong devotion to Methodism was laid here among the town's passionate African American congregants. Despite a number of zealous white Methodist missionaries circulating in the coastal regions of North and South Carolina, Methodism was unpopular with most whites in that area at the turn of

---

the Practice," in George A. Singleton, ed., *The Life Experience and Gospel Labors of the Rt. Rev. Richard Allen* (Nashville, Tenn.: Abingdon Press, 1960), 70.

9. The following works deal with various facets of slave life in the Lower Cape Fear in the late eighteenth and early nineteenth centuries: Catherine Bishir, "Black Builders in Antebellum North Carolina," *North Carolina Historical Review* 61 (October 1984), 422–61; James H. Brewer, "An Account of Negro Slavery in the Cape Fear Region Prior to 1860" (Ph.D. dissertation, University of Pittsburgh, 1949); James M. Clifton, "Golden Grains of White: Rice Planting on the Lower Cape Fear," *North Carolina Historical Review* 50 (October 1973), 365–93; Lawrence Lee, *The Lower Cape Fear in Colonial Days* (Chapel Hill: University of North Carolina Press, 1965).

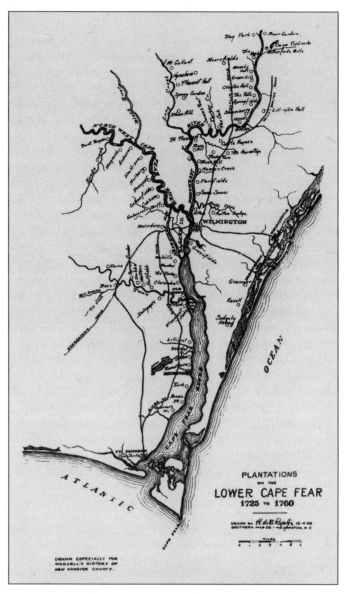

Map of the Lower Cape Fear region of North Carolina, where David Walker spent the earliest years of his life. From Alfred Moore Waddell, *A History of New Hanover County and the Lower Cape Fear Region*, vol. 1 (n.d.). (Courtesy New Hanover County Public Library)

the century because of its persisting, though weakening, antislavery position. Many referred to it as the "Nigger religion" because slaves in the region flocked to listen to the preachers who braved grave abuse to spread their creed. Thus, with only minimal support from a handful of local whites, blacks in Wilmington largely created the denomination in that town, and "African stewards" oversaw its administration into the early nineteenth century. By then, however, the church was accommodating to Southern realities and had disavowed its previous mandate that members free their slaves. By 1810 the administration of the local church had been taken over by whites, whose numbers in the denomination throughout the South were growing rapidly. Yet blacks in Wilmington continued to be closely allied with the church.[10] The vitality of life in Wilmington was absolutely dependent on black talents and initiative. Indeed, this reality shaped early-nineteenth-century town life all along the southeastern seaboard of the United States.[11] The young and keen Walker could not have missed this fact, or failed to discern the paradox of such powerful people living as slaves.

American slavery was brutal, and Wilmington was no exception. Slaves often ran away from the harsh regimen of labor in rice swamps and pine barrens and hid in the swamps pervading this low-lying country. A number of them formed makeshift communities in these fastnesses and supplied and even armed themselves with goods, animals, and weapons taken from nearby plantations. Some even shot particularly vicious overseers and owners. A slave leader named "the General of the Swamps" and his followers comprised just such a force in the Wilmington region in the mid-

10. For a fuller discussion of early Methodism in Wilmington and the Lower Cape Fear, see Hinks, *To Awaken My Afflicted Brethren*, 15–20.

11. For a sampling of work on urban slave life along the southern seaboard, see Tommy L. Bogger, *Free Blacks in Norfolk, Virginia, 1790–1860: The Darker Side of Freedom* (Charlottesville: University of Virginia Press, 1997); Douglas Egerton, *Gabriel's Rebellion: The Virginia Slave Conspiracies of 1800 and 1802* (Chapel Hill: University of North Carolina Press, 1993); Philip Morgan, "Black Life in Eighteenth-Century Charleston," *Perspectives in American History*, new series, 1 (1984), 185–222; Christopher Phillips, *Freedom's Port: The African American Community of Baltimore, 1790–1860* (Urbana: University of Illinois Press, 1997).

1790s, alarming whites until they were subdued in 1795. When such outliers—as they were called—were captured, the most infamous were often summarily executed, after which their severed heads were placed on long poles that were displayed prominently on a point of land directly across the Cape Fear River from the town's main wharves, brazenly called "Nigger Head Point" by locals. The rotting heads could only have represented for Walker the very heart of race and labor relations in the Slave South.

The lower Cape Fear region was by no means the only area in the early-nineteenth-century South where African Americans resisted their enslavement. Indeed, a great slave restlessness was apparent all along the southeastern seaboard during this era. From the American Revolution through the end of the century, slaves—spurred by the examples of whites waging an anticolonial struggle and by the opportunities the Revolution's disruption created—struck repeatedly against their subjugation in Virginia, North and South Carolina, and Georgia. For example, slaves armed by Virginia's royal governor, Lord Dunmore, in late 1775 formed their own regiment and battled with local slaveholders around Williamsburg. Slaves in Georgia who had fought with the British could not be removed by state authorities from their fortifications along the Savannah River until 1786, well after the Revolution's end.[12]

The dawning of the new century heralded increased and better organized slave resistance and conspiracies. In 1800,

12. For a thorough overview of these and other events, see Herbert Aptheker, *American Negro Slave Revolts*, 5th ed. (New York: International Publishers, 1983), 196–208; Jeffrey J. Crow, "Slave Rebelliousness and Social Conflict in North Carolina, 1775–1802," *William and Mary Quarterly*, 3rd ser., 37 (1980), 79–102; Sylvia Frey, *Water from the Rock: Black Resistance in a Revolutionary Age* (Princeton: Princeton University Press, 1991); Hinks, *To Awaken My Afflicted Brethren*, 40–47; R. H. Taylor, "Slave Conspiracies in North Carolina," *North Carolina Historical Review* 5 (January 1928), 20–34; Alan D. Watson, "Impulse Toward Independence: Resistance and Rebellion Among North Carolina Slaves, 1750–1775," *Journal of Negro History* 63 (1978), 317–28; Peter H. Wood, " 'The Dream Deferred': Black Freedom Struggles on the Eve of Independence," in Gary Y. Okihiro, ed., *In Resistance: Studies in African, Caribbean, and Afro-American History* (Amherst: University of Massachusetts Press, 1986), 166–87.

an enslaved blacksmith named Gabriel, who lived near Richmond and who sought to realize the civic and economic freedom promised to white men by the Revolution, joined with a number of similarly inspired confederates to strike against slavery in Virginia. They took advantage of deep political fissures then existing among local white Federalists and Jeffersonian Republicans to orchestrate a conspiracy of hundreds of slaves that spread over many of the state's counties. On the night of 30 August 1800, they planned to attack Richmond from various points, and would probably have done so had not a torrential rainstorm washed out all the bridges as the rebels massed outside the town. While this conspiracy failed, its momentum led to further organizing among slaves in southeastern Virginia and northeastern North Carolina, which fostered a number of plots and small uprisings in the region in 1801 and 1802. Although, once again, none was successful in mounting a rebellion or threatening slavery, the statement of one rebel—"They shall know the birth of liberty is as free for us as for themselves"—made vivid to local slaveholders the aspirations and restlessness of many of their human chattel and filled many with dread.[13] Walker's *Appeal* would swell with this spirit.

All these incidents were also influenced by a religious revivalism, then sweeping the Upper South, that provided an opportunity for whites and blacks to gather together in large numbers and hear enthused evangelicals preach about the spiritual equality of all through Christ, a message with a potentially inflammatory secular meaning. These highly emotional camp meetings could challenge the boundaries of conventional racial etiquette and give restive slaves seeking an end to racial inequality further justification for their cause. This restlessness would continue in eastern North Carolina throughout the early decades of the nineteenth century and could not have eluded the notice of Walker.[14]

13. Letter from J.L.C., Slave Collection, 1787–1856, File "Transcripts, Conspiracy 1802," North Carolina State Archives, Raleigh.

14. For further discussions of these and related events, see Merton Dillon, *Slavery Attacked: Southern Slaves and Their Allies, 1619–1865* (Baton Rouge: Louisiana State University Press, 1990), 97–103; Egerton, *Gabriel's Rebellion*; Hinks, *To Awaken My Afflicted Brethren*, 47–61; Rhys Isaac, "Evan-

Sometime in the 1810s, Walker journeyed to Charleston, South Carolina. Again no record of the time he spent there exists, but he did refer in the *Appeal* to riding a steamboat to a religious revival outside Charleston. This probably occurred on or about 1821, because steamboats had then been navigating Charleston's rivers for only a few years and 1821 was also the first year boats visited the site of this particular camp meeting. Charleston would have attracted Walker because of its vastly larger free black population (3,615 in 1820), far greater employment opportunities, and numerous black organizations.[15] Perhaps the most important of these organizations for Walker was the new AME congregation that a number of the town's black religious leaders formed in 1817 after Richard Allen and his associates founded the denomination in Philadelphia in 1816. Its establishment in Charleston was greeted immediately as threatening by white authorities, who labored for the next five years to close it.[16]

Having first been nurtured in the rich black Methodism of Wilmington, David Walker's devotion to evangelical Christianity deepened through his likely association with this Charleston church. Here Walker began his adulation of Richard Allen, whom he believed was "among the greatest divines who have lived since the apostolic age." He was con-

---

gelical Revolt: The Nature of the Baptists' Challenge to the Traditional Order in Virginia, 1765–1775," *William and Mary Quarterly*, 3rd ser., 31 (1974), 345–68; Gerald W. Mullin, *Flight and Rebellion: Slave Resistance in Eighteenth-Century Virginia* (New York: Oxford University Press, 1972).

15. Regarding slave and free black life in early-nineteenth-century Charleston, see: Ira Berlin, *Slaves Without Masters: The Free Negro in the Antebellum South* (New York: Pantheon Books, 1974); Hinks, *To Awaken My Afflicted Brethren*, 22–30; Michael P. Johnson and James L. Roark, *Black Masters: A Free Family of Color in the Old South* (New York: W. W. Norton & Co., 1984); Marina Wikramanayake, *A World in Shadow: The Free Black in Antebellum South Carolina* (Columbia: University of South Carolina Press, 1973).

16. Regarding Richard Allen and the origins of the African Methodist Episcopal Church, see Carol V. R. George, *Segregated Sabbaths: Richard Allen and the Rise of Independent Black Churches, 1760–1840* (New York: Oxford University Press, 1973). Concerning the AME church in Charleston, see Hinks, *To Awaken My Afflicted Brethren*, 25–30.

vinced Allen would be the savior of African America.[17] Walker also learned how much an independent black church could challenge planter hegemony by affording African Americans a vital institution under their own control and a forum for interpreting Scripture based on their own experience and aspirations.

The famous conspiracy of Denmark Vesey issued from the social controversy swirling about the church. Denmark Vesey, a successful free black carpenter who had been a slave through his early adult years, was an impassioned member of the new church and was with numerous of his congregants deeply embittered when local authorities moved against the African Church, as it was called. This constant harassment, coupled with their hatred of slavery and of gross racial inequities, led Vesey and such similarly devout associates as Jack Pritchard, Peter Poyas, and Ned and Rolla Bennett, to consider an insurrection as early as 1818. By early 1822, talk had shifted to more concrete plans to rally slaves from the surrounding rice parishes to attack the city at the same time slaves and free blacks in Charleston would raid the arsenal and set fires at strategic points. They organized extensively and planned to strike at some point in June, but at the last moment an informant revealed the plot to authorities and the leaders were seized and soon hanged.[18]

Walker was very likely exposed to this series of events, if not a participant of some sort in the plot. The African Church and the depth of support it summoned in black

17. *Appeal*, 61.
18. Some of the best works dealing with the Denmark Vesey Conspiracy are: Douglas R. Egerton, *"He Shall Go Out Free": The Lives of Denmark Vesey* (Madison, Wis.: Madison House, 1999); William Freehling, *Prelude to the Civil War: The Nullification Controversy in South Carolina, 1816–1836* (New York: Harper & Row, 1966), 49–86; Richard C. Wade, "The Vesey Plot: A Reconsideration," *Journal of Southern History* 30 (May 1964), 143–61; Wikramanayake, *A World in Shadow*. There are also excellent collections of documents on the plot: John Oliver Killens, ed., *The Trial Record of Denmark Vesey* (Boston: Beacon Press, 1970); Edward A. Pearson, *Designs Against Charleston: The Trial Record of the Denmark Vesey Slave Conspiracy of 1822* (Chapel Hill: University of North Carolina Press, 1999); Robert S. Starobin, *Denmark Vesey: The Slave Conspiracy of 1822* (Englewood Cliffs, N.J.: Prentice-Hall, 1970).

Charlestonians must have helped convince Walker that religion would prove decisive in charging African Americans with an appreciation of their worth as individuals and as a people, and with the courage to strike against their oppression. In Charleston, African Americans proved willing to die to protect their faith and to improve their freedom. Walker would fill his *Appeal* with evangelical fervor in hopes of promoting and preserving that conviction.

Probably sometime soon after the Vesey affair, Walker's journey through America resumed. Key free black figures in the Charleston church—such as the Reverend Morris Brown, Henry Drayton, and Charles Corr, who had not been linked directly with the plot but who authorities suspected were sympathizers—were banished from the town as soon as the conspiracy was uncovered. Many other free blacks followed in their wake as the church was razed once and for all and reaction and martial law gripped the town. It would be no surprise if Walker had been among them.

In the *Appeal*, Walker attested that he had "travelled over a considerable portion of these United States," but where exactly he did not say.[19] Perhaps he went south to Georgia and Alabama and made his way up the Mississippi from New Orleans. Maybe he visited such western states as Kentucky and Ohio. More likely he headed north to a city like Philadelphia—a common way station for blacks coming from the South, the center for the AME church, and the destination of Morris Brown and numerous other Charleston refugees.[20] There might also have been a sojourn in New York City or Baltimore, because both cities had large and active black communities.[21] But wherever his travels took him, they only

19. *Appeal*, 3.
20. Regarding free black life in antebellum Philadelphia, see Nash, *Forging Freedom*, and Julie Winch, *Philadelphia's Black Elite: Activism, Accommodation, and the Struggle for Autonomy, 1787–1848* (Philadelphia: Temple University Press, 1988).
21. Regarding slave and free black life in early-nineteenth-century Baltimore and New York City, see Phillips, *Freedom's Port*, and Shane White, *Somewhat More Independent: The End of Slavery in New York City, 1770–1810* (Athens: University of Georgia Press, 1991).

strengthened his "unshaken conviction" that African Americans "are the most wretched, degraded, and abject set of beings that ever lived since the world began."[22]

By 1825, Walker had settled in Boston: he appeared in the City Directory for that year and every following year until his death in 1830.[23] He quickly established a small used-clothing business, an enterprise that more and more local blacks were entering in the latter years of the 1820s.[24] By February 1826, Walker had married Eliza Butler, a local woman, and by July of the same year he had been initiated into Prince Hall, or African, Masonry at Boston's famous African Lodge #459.[25] He also joined a local black Methodist church shepherded by the fiery and beloved antislavery minister Samuel Snowden, who after 1831 became a key ally of William Lloyd Garrison, one of the founders of the new American abolitionism. Walker and Snowden became fast friends.[26]

In the short space of two years, Walker had risen significantly in prominence in black Boston and had become an important community activist. He was the principal agent in Boston for the first black newspaper in the United States,

22. *Appeal*, 3, 9.

23. *The Boston Directory*, 1825, comp. Charles Stimpson Jr. et al. (Boston, 1825).

24. For a fuller discussion of Walker's years in Boston, see Hinks, *To Awaken My Afflicted Brethren*, 63–115.

25. Prince Hall was a Methodist minister and the principal leader of Boston's free blacks in the late eighteenth century. He was born in Barbados in 1735 and arrived a slave in Boston in the 1740s. In 1787, Hall founded African Masonry in Boston after local white Masons refused to accept a charter earlier issued to him from a British lodge once they also refused to admit him and his brothers into their lodge. African Masonry grew in the Northeast in the early decades of the nineteenth century and fostered communication among regional black leaders. It also provided vital sinews for fledgling free black communities. For fuller treatments of Hall and his significance, see Lorenzo Greene, "Prince Hall: Massachusetts Leader in Crisis," *Freedomways* 1 (Fall 1961), 238–58, and Sidney and Emma Nogrady Kaplan, *The Black Presence in the Era of the American Revolution*, rev. ed. (Amherst: University of Massachusetts Press, 1989), 202–14.

26. Regarding Snowden, his church, and his relationship to David Walker, see Hinks, *To Awaken My Afflicted Brethren*, 78–79.

Freedom's Journal, and he rallied critical support for it in its early months in 1827.[27] Along with his fellow lodge brothers, he helped organize and police several parades, or "African Celebrations," on Beacon Hill's north slope in the late 1820s. These parades were major annual events for black Boston and celebrated the independence of Haiti in 1804 and emancipation in Massachusetts. Walker gave the keynote address at one of them, which honored the visit to Boston of an African prince, Abduhhl Rahhaman, recently manumitted in the South.[28]

Walker may also have been the prime mover in the creation of one of the first avowedly black political organizations in America, the Massachusetts General Colored Association (MGCA). Although by the 1820s such institutions as the Prince Hall Masons and the AME had lodges and churches in various towns in the Northeast and Middle Atlantic, which helped to interconnect the leaders of different communities and to foster some regional identity of interest, the various branches remained overwhelmingly local in focus and shunned political activity. What made the MGCA so significant and different from the Prince Hall Masons and the AME was its pronouncement of new objectives for African Americans: to promote aggressively and publicly the abolition of slavery and the intellectual and moral improvement of blacks in America, and to do so by encouraging African Americans to join together in one body, not just in Massachusetts but throughout the nation. This was a radical departure for African Americans and evinced their mounting political confidence in the North by the late 1820s. And it was David Walker who articulated this new assertiveness best when he addressed the Association in December 1828: "The primary object of this institution is to unite the colored population, so far, through the United

27. For a fuller discussion of this critically important newspaper and its immediate offspring, *The Rights of All,* see Bella Gross, "*Freedom's Journal* and the *Rights of All,*" *Journal of Negro History* 17 (1932), 241–86.

28. Regarding the interesting history of this fascinating individual, see Terry Alford, *Prince Among Slaves* (New York: Harcourt Brace Jovanovich, 1977).

States . . . and not [withhold] anything which may have the least tendency to meliorate *our* miserable condition."[29]

"Why are the Americans so very fearfully terrified respecting my Book?": The Meaning of Walker's *Appeal*

David Walker's zeal to redress the horrible injustices perpetrated on African Americans joined with his oratorical eloquence and passion and propelled his rapid rise to prominence. By 1829, black Boston increasingly delegated to him the authority to express its deepest-held sorrow, anger, and aspirations. Later that year, in September, David Walker published the first edition of his *Appeal to the Coloured Citizens of the World,* one of the most neglected yet most important political and social documents of the nineteenth century. No one was surprised to read in the *Boston Evening Transcript* that the response of the black community to Walker's words was that "they glory in its principles, as if it were a star in the east, guiding them to freedom and emancipation."[30]

Displaying a vehemence and outrage unprecedented among contemporary African American authors, Walker's *Appeal* decried in vivid and personal terms the uniquely savage, unchristian treatment blacks suffered in the United States, especially as slaves:

> We Coloured People of these United States, are, the most wretched, degraded and abject set of beings that ever lived since the world began, down to the present day, and, that, the white Christians of America, who hold us in slavery, (or, more properly speaking, pretenders to Christianity,) treat us more cruel and barba-

29. *Freedom's Journal,* 19 December 1828. Reprinted in the Appendix, Document II, 85.

30. *Boston Evening Transcript,* 28 September 1830. Reprinted in the Appendix, Document X, 109.

rous than any Heathen nation did any people whom it had subjected.[31]

By brutally enslaving African Americans and by depriving them of secular education, the word of God, civil liberties, and any position of social responsibility, white Americans had forced blacks closer and closer to the life of brutes. Under such an onus, it was no surprise to Walker that African Americans had become demoralized and apparently resigned to the social mudsill white society assigned them.

But even more insidious in impact was the pervasive belief among whites that blacks were physically, intellectually, and morally inferior to white Americans, a conviction that was a critical element in justifications for subjugation of African Americans. Walker excoriated this most "insupportable insult" that whites hurled at blacks: that "they were not of the human family" but descended originally "from the tribes of *Monkeys* or *Orang-Outangs*."[32] For Walker, Thomas Jefferson—author of the Declaration of Independence, third President of the United States, and a most eloquent defender of an egalitarian republicanism—also was the nation's most effective proponent of that belief. In his famous *Notes on the State of Virginia*, Jefferson characterized blacks as physically far less attractive than whites, full of a sexual impulsiveness detached from love, prone to lethargy when not employed, "dull, tasteless, and anomalous" in their imagination, and far below whites in the capacity to reason.[33] He stressed that their proximity to whites had had little tendency to improve them and thus conjectured:

> Blacks, whether originally a distinct race, or made distinct by time and circumstances, are inferior to the whites in the endowments both of body and mind. It is not against experience to suppose, that different species of the same genus, or varieties of the same species,

31. *Appeal*, 2.
32. *Appeal*, 12.
33. All of the following quoted material comes from Thomas Jefferson, *Notes on the State of Virginia*, ed. William Peden (Chapel Hill: University of North Carolina Press, 1954), 137–43.

> may possess different qualifications. Will not a lover of
> natural history then, one who views the gradations in all
> the races of animals with the eye of philosophy, excuse
> an effort to keep those in the department of man as
> distinct as nature has formed them? This unfortunate
> difference of colour, and perhaps of faculty, is a power-
> ful obstacle to the emancipation of these people.

Because of this comprehensive inferiority, wrote Jefferson,
if blacks are to be freed they must "be removed beyond the
reach of mixture" with whites because of the inevitable conflict that will ensue from this divide in abilities and thus the
grave threat blacks would pose to white America's noble ex-
periment with democracy.

Although outraged at such scurrilous speculations,
Walker also recognized that they were given enormous cred-
ibility because they had been uttered by as great a national
luminary as Jefferson.

> Do you know that Mr. Jefferson was one of as great char-
> acters as ever lived among the whites? See his writings
> for the world, and public labours for the United States
> of America. Do you believe that the assertions of such a
> man, will pass away into oblivion unobserved by this
> people and the world? If you do you are much mis-
> taken— . . . I say, that unless we try to refute Mr. Jeffer-
> son's arguments respecting us, we will only establish
> them.[34]

Walker believed that one of the most urgent assignments for
African Americans now was to attack and refute this nefari-
ous doctrine, because it was the ideological centerpiece of
American racism.

By the late 1820s, antiblack ideology was becoming more
aggressive and gaining greater favor among whites, and
these key writings of Jefferson only sanctioned this mounting racial antipathy. The American Colonization Society
(ACS), created in late 1816 to promote and facilitate the re-

34. *Appeal*, 17–18.

moval of the nation's free blacks to a site in Africa, generally relied on highly negative characterizations of blacks—such as Jefferson employed—to justify their call for removal and they refused to fight racial discrimination in the United States.[35] While a handful of more "enlightened" members argued that removing free blacks to Africa would allow them to avoid the entrenched and unfair barriers that prejudice placed in their way in America—thus putting much of the blame for the predicament of blacks not on them but on white racism—the overwhelming majority of white colonizationists agreed that free blacks should leave because of their inherent inferiority and because of the problems they themselves created for white republican America. A common characterization viewed them as "notoriously ignorant, degraded and miserable, mentally diseased, brokenspirited, acted upon by no motive to honourable exertions, scarcely reached in their debasement by the heavenly light, . . . indolent, abject and sorrowful." As the ACS gained enormous popularity among whites in the 1820s, these attitudes toward blacks gained greater currency and legitimacy as well.

These attitudes served another important ideological function in that decade as well. Political democracy for white males was expanding greatly then as numerous states in the North wrote new constitutions and eliminated property requirements for voting. Yet as the white electorate grew significantly, that of blacks diminished inversely as such states as New Jersey, Pennsylvania, New York, and Connecticut wrote laws either proscribing black suffrage altogether or else placing great property and residential restrictions on it. Whites in the North were nearly unanimous in their belief that blacks were unfit to vote, and applauded these new laws

---

35. Regarding the roots, history, and ideological orientations of the American Colonization Society, see Douglas Egerton, " 'Its Origin Is Not a Little Curious': A New Look at the American Colonization Society," *Journal of the Early Republic* 5 (Winter 1985), 463–80; George Fredrickson, *The Black Image in the White Mind: The Debate on Afro-American Character and Destiny, 1817–1914* (New York: Harper & Row, 1971), 1–32; Philip Staudenraus, *The African Colonization Movement, 1816–1865* (New York: Columbia University Press, 1961).

despite the protests of notable blacks, such as Philadelphia's James Forten.[36] African Americans were also routinely discriminated against in the North in all public facilities related to transport, housing, eating, schooling, worship, and justice. Only in Massachusetts could black males serve as jurors, and all states placed restrictions on the use of black testimony in court. Most Northern states also maintained irregularly enforced laws strictly regulating or forbidding altogether the immigration of free blacks into their states. As David Walker was writing his *Appeal*, racism and the ideology justifying it seemed to be becoming only more virulent and popular.

Fueling this momentum, ironically, was the growing assertiveness and political confidence of African Americans. By the 1820s, the communities of blacks in Northern cities, such as Boston, New York, Philadelphia, and elsewhere, had grown in numbers and had built an institutional infrastructure through churches, schools, and mutual-aid societies and developed a cadre of increasingly confident leaders.[37] One of the most important ways in which African Americans manifested their new assertiveness and commitment to be local and national political actors was in their pervasive opposition to the objectives and ideology of the ACS, articulated the most effectively by Walker—one of the new leaders—in his *Appeal*. They revealed precisely the capacity and will to participate politically that the burgeoning racial ideology proclaimed they did not and could not have. Thus this ideology acquired the vehemence it did by the late 1820s in part because the evidence from blacks refuting it was so apparent and had to be attacked aggressively. White-

36. See, for example, selections from James Forten's 1813 *Letters from a Man of Colour on a Late Bill Before the Senate of Pennsylvania*, which protested against measures currently being considered in the state legislature to check the flow of African American migrants into the city. The selections are contained in Gary Nash, *Race and Revolution* (Madison, Wis.: Madison House, 1990), 190–98. Works treating antiblack legislation and discrimination in the North more generally are Leonard P. Curry, *The Free Black in Urban America, 1800–1850: The Shadow of the Dream* (Chicago: University of Chicago Press, 1981), and Leon Litwack, *North of Slavery: The Negro in the Free States, 1790–1860* (Chicago: University of Chicago Press, 1961).

37. See, for example, Hinks, *To Awaken My Afflicted Brethren*, 91–115.

ness was designated by definition as superior to blackness
and a realm that had to be protected from *any* intermixture
with the inferior race by firm boundaries. During this period, white mob violence against these black enclaves grew,
and it would only proliferate in the early 1830s as blacks in
the North and a handful of whites organized to form very
outspoken societies for the abolition of slavery and seemed
intent upon erasing the barriers separating white from
black.[38]

Walker was certain that upholding all this was the sophisticated racism of Thomas Jefferson, and he set his sights accordingly.

> For my own part, I am glad Mr. Jefferson has advanced
> his positions for your sake; for you will either have to
> contradict or confirm him by your own actions, and not
> by what our friends have said or done for us; . . . Mr.
> Jefferson's remarks respecting us, have sunk deep into
> the hearts of millions of the whites, and never will be
> removed this side of eternity.—For how can they, when
> we are confirming him every day, by our *groveling sub-
> missions* and *treachery*?[39]

Walker was afraid that the pervasive indictment of black
character spawned by Jefferson's words might profoundly
demoralize African Americans, and he wanted the *Appeal* to
be a contrary clarion to them of their worth as humans, their
noble history in Africa, and God's special love for them.
Walker's *Appeal* challenged African Americans to lift themselves up and organize to cast off this oppression, which, he
proclaimed, God found an intolerable provocation and sin-
ful for them to endure any longer: "Your full glory and hap-

38. For an illuminating analysis of these events and the troubling racial
bifurcation of the American North in the 1830s, see James B. Stewart, "The
Emergence of Racial Modernity and the Rise of the White North, 1790–
1840," *Journal of the Early Republic* 18 (Summer 1998), 181–217. The best
general treatment of antiabolitionist mobs in the 1830s remains Leonard
L. Richards, *"Gentlemen of Property and Standing": Anti-Abolition Mobs in Jack-
sonian America* (New York: Oxford University Press, 1970).

39. *Appeal*, 30.

piness . . . under Heaven, shall never be fully consummated, but with the *entire emancipation of your enslaved brethren all over the world*."[40]

Despite America's horrible sins, Walker proclaimed, the nation was fully redeemable, and he refused to abandon it. America must be held to the high ideals embodied in Boston's State House and in Winthrop's vision of American exemplariness—but African Americans must be embraced as intrinsic participants in this mission. The American promise of liberty, equality, learning, and boundless opportunity must be preserved, but slavery, racial discrimination, and theories of racial inferiority must be abjured and extirpated root and branch. That was the stain of America that Walker refused to hide any longer, and instead exposed to "the eyes of all people" to shame them and wither it. He hoped to regenerate the nation through the Christian convictions of Americans and to restore it to its highest ideals.

> Throw away your fears and prejudices then, and enlighten us and treat us like men, and we will like you more than we do now hate you. . . . Treat us like men, and there is no danger but we will all live in peace and happiness together. For we are not like you, hard hearted, unmerciful, and unforgiving. What a happy country this will be, if the whites will listen. What nation under heaven, will be able to do anything with us, unless God gives us up into its hand? . . . Treat us then like men, and we will be your friends. And there is not a doubt in my mind, but that the whole of the past will be sunk into oblivion, and we yet, under God, will become a united and happy people.[41]

Walker used England as an example of a nation of whites that he fully embraced because of their historic philanthropy toward blacks by ending their key involvement with the Atlantic slave trade earlier in the century and at present agitating aggressively for an end to slavery altogether in their

40. *Appeal*, 32.
41. *Appeal*, 73.

colonies. A nation that in the eighteenth century had been the Atlantic's most aggressive promoter of African slavery had transformed itself and forsworn trafficking in Africans, evincing the capacity of whites to regenerate themselves, while also suggesting that, ironically, the British might be the true defenders of the liberty and equality enshrined by the American Revolution against that same nation fifty years earlier. "The English are the best friends the coloured people have upon earth," Walker proclaimed in 1830. "They are the greatest benefactors we have."[42] Such benevolence from white Americans would prompt a similarly warm reception from Walker and spur the national racial reconciliation he still believed was possible.

As Walker was circulating his pamphlet in early 1829, religious revivals were sweeping the Northeast, especially in regions undergoing rapid economic change, such as New York's Erie Canal corridor.[43] These revivals stimulated tens of thousands of individual conversions and promoted widespread fervor for the arrival of the Christian millennium, the thousand-year era during which Christ would return to reign on earth and social harmony would prevail. Many were convinced that it was America's unique mission to take the

42. *Appeal*, 43. Such passages, however, are not meant to suggest that Walker was unaware of Britain's persisting and brutal involvement with slavery in the West Indies, especially Jamaica. See his footnote in *Appeal*, 66n. He also knew full well how the English subjugated the Irish in their own isles. See *Appeal*, 9. Part of the testament to Walker's extensive learning was his remarkable appreciation for the complexities of politics and society in the Atlantic world in 1830. Nevertheless, with regard to issues pertinent specifically to African Americans, he designated real humanitarian advances made by the British and their abolitionist luminaries, such as Thomas Clarkson, William Wilberforce, and Granville Sharp, and upheld that nation—still deeply resented and feared by most white Americans—as a challenge to Americans to fulfill their commitment to the ideals of the Revolution and Christianity. For a brilliant discussion of the complex relationship that David Walker and abolitionists in Boston had with England, see James B. Stewart, "Boston, Abolition, and the Atlantic World, 1820–1861," in Donald Jacobs, ed., *Courage and Conscience: Black and White Abolitionists in Boston* (Bloomington: Indiana University Press, 1993), 101–25.

43. See, for example, Paul E. Johnson, *A Shopkeeper's Millennium: Society and Revivals in Rochester, New York, 1815–1837* (New York: Hill & Wang, 1978).

lead in ushering in this millennium, a belief that had roots
in Winthrop's vision and the pronouncements of countless
clerics following him. After converting to one of the evangelical faiths supporting the revivals, people were encouraged
to live more godly lives by, for example, forswearing the use
of alcohol and oaths, refusing to work on the Sabbath, distributing tracts to the unconverted, and proselytizing. The
new abolitionism of the 1830s, which mandated the immediate and unqualified emancipation of the slaves, drew as well
on this millennial impulse.[44] The hope was that by so re-
forming one's life the onset of the millennium would be
brought that much closer. Walker believed deeply in this
millennial mission of America, and he was filled with similar
enthusiasm for the popular revivals. He was certain that
until offending white Americans made heartfelt repentance
to God for their crimes against blacks, and until every African American renounced slavishness and worked actively to
abolish slavery and racism, the arrival of the millennium
would be forestalled and, indeed, their failure instead bring
down the fearsome wrath of God. As he wrote at the opening
of his work:

> The day of our redemption from abject wretchedness
> draweth near, when we shall be enabled, in the most
> extended sense of the word, to stretch forth our hands
> to the LORD our GOD, but there must be a willingness
> on our part, for GOD to do these things for us, for we
> may be assured that he will not take us by the hairs of
> our head against our will and desire, and drag us from
> our very, mean, low and abject condition.[45]

God demanded a devout and fearless activism from those
roused by his saving grace.

At times, however, it appears that Walker argued against

---

44. The two best general treatments of abolitionism in America after
1830 are: James B. Stewart, *Holy Warriors: The Abolitionists and American Slavery*, 2nd ed. (New York: Hill & Wang, 1996), and Ronald Walters, *The Antislavery Appeal: American Abolitionism After 1830* (New York: W. W. Norton &
Co., 1978).

45. *Appeal*, 2.

activism, counseling African Americans instead to await the arrival of some divinely appointed savior of the race. At one point he declared: "[God] will give you a Hannibal" whom African Americans should support fully, and God will then "deliver you through him from your deplorable and wretched condition."[46] On several other occasions, Walker warned of imminent judgment from God independent of any action taken by blacks. Nevertheless, the burden of Walker's assertions evince his conviction that blacks must not wait for someone else to seize for them "our freedom which God has given us."[47] Time and again he urged all blacks that "there is a great work for you to do" and that they must not delay its commencement. While finally God's actions were not contingent, Walker seemed certain that the benevolent transformation of the world—indeed, the very arrival of the millennium—would never occur without the initiative of God's saved.

Walker hoped that this holy activism would regenerate the nation and that African Americans who in 1829 seemed so outside of America, who were defined by whites as so threatening to America and its mission, could yet be peaceably incorporated into it and share in its responsibilities and benefits fully with whites. Indeed, he believed that God would use African Americans, not white Americans, as the spearhead of the Christianization of the world.[48] Individual repentance, reformation, and activism were the keys to transforming a wayward America, Walker believed, and the *Appeal* was structured to prompt this renovation, especially of African Americans. According to Walker, the source of America's horrible problems with race and slavery was not in the nation's systems and institutions but in the hearts of Americans. Slavery was an abominable aberration in a society that was otherwise healthy and even morally righteous. He lauded the individual freedom and equality enshrined in the Declaration of Independence while excoriating the nation for excluding African Americans from its promises.

46. *Appeal*, 22.
47. *Appeal*, 14n.
48. *Appeal*, 20n.

Rather than indicting the fundamental values and principles of American society for endorsing a pursuit of individual liberty and profit that could be so immoral that it legitimized such a gross exploitation of labor as slavery, Walker believed that unchristian hypocrites had flourished in America's historically unique freedom and perverted to their own cruel, avaricious, and selfish ends the values of liberty and equality that actually formed the hope that was America. These hypocrites would ultimately either be weeded out by God or made productive, virtuous citizens through Christian regeneration. Thus, Walker's faith in the core values of antebellum America—freedom, individual improvement, economic opportunity, and Protestant mission—enabled him to attack the nation without abandoning it, and to that extent made him less of a threat.

Such deep individual change would prove critical in renovating the nation, as would the frank encounter Walker prescribed for the nation with the reality of its racial crimes. Yet Walker's faith in the comprehensive efficacy of individual regeneration and the inevitability of the millennium led him to overlook the deep systemic problems that slavery and racism posed for America. He held that spiritual regeneration would render race incidental and be supplanted by an abiding current of Christian connectedness among all Americans. Yet from America's beginnings in the early seventeenth century, race served as one of the land's most central signifiers and would not easily cede dominion, even in the realm of religion. An ideology explaining and justifying racial inequality in America, and the judicial, political, economic, and social policies emanating from it, were at the very foundation of American society and would be nothing other than imposing in their intractability. The Southern economy was absolutely founded on enslaved black labor. While slavery had been all but eliminated in the North by 1829, antipathy among whites against any sign of racial equality pervaded the entire region and would only become more aggressive in the 1830s. A host of laws and legal decisions reflected and extended these racial foundations of the nation and created exclusively for whites many vital rights and privileges that they would refuse to forgo, based on the belief that the di-

vinely created natural inferiority of people of African descent entitled whites, who were in the vast majority, to these
privileges. Against these deep-set details of the daily work-
ings of racism in antebellum America, Walker would need to
bring much more to bear than merely a call for individual
spiritual regeneration, especially because, as Walker himself
makes clear in the *Appeal*, religious worship and theology in
America—North and South—were infused with racism and
the Bible was variously drawn on to justify it.

> The wicked and ungodly, seeing their preachers treat
> us with so much cruelty, they say: our preachers, who
> must be right, if any body are, treat them like brutes,
> and why cannot we?—They think it is no harm to keep
> them in slavery and put the whip to them, and why can-
> not we do the same!—They being preachers of the gos-
> pel of Jesus Christ, if it were any harm, they would
> surely preach against their oppression and do their ut-
> most to erase it from the country . . . and would cease
> only with the complete overthrow of the system of slav-
> ery, in every part of the country.[49]

But of course he knew they did not. Racial inequality was
embedded inextricably in antebellum America, and Walker's
proposals for transformation seem not to grapple with that
reality as fully as they needed to.

But this is in no way to suggest that Walker was unaware
that white regeneration well might *not* occur, and that the
racial brutality he so vividly described would only continue
to prosper in America. Indeed, throughout his work he referred to whites as the "natural enemies" of blacks. Although
he did not think they were natural enemies "from the beginning" or that such a condition precluded reconciliation,
Walker did believe that whites' unremittingly savage physical abuse of blacks and their assignment of blacks to biblical
infamy through God's curse of Cain and to a biological inferiority to Europeans, had by the nineteenth century rendered them such. Many of these whites, Walker warned,

---

49. *Appeal*, 40–41.

"have gone so far that their cup must be filled," and God will damn them, even though, he added significantly, "I should like to see the whites repent peradventure God may have mercy on them."[50] Yet many would fail to do so. Substantial change would be difficult for both blacks and whites, especially for the latter, and if it failed to transpire, blacks must still refuse to submit further to this degradation of them. Walker asserted that the apocalyptic destruction of a redeemable society was commanded by God if it failed to heed his warnings.

> Remember Americans, that we must and shall be free and enlightened as you are, will you wait until we shall, under God, obtain our liberty by the crushing arm of power? Will it not be dreadful for you? I speak Americans for your good. We must and shall be free I say, in spite of you. You may do your best to keep us in wretchedness and misery, to enrich you and your children; but God will deliver us from under you. And wo, wo, will be to you if we have to obtain our freedom by fighting.[51]

While Walker clearly feared the consequences of open racial warfare, he declared that God mandated such a cataclysm rather than tolerate any further truckling of blacks with servility. The *Appeal*, while offering hope for interracial fellowship, upheld even more the reasonableness of black rage and God's stern judgment, with the intention of preparing African Americans for waging the horrible racial battle they well might have to undertake. No other document produced by white or black from the nineteenth century communicated this reality and this awful responsibility so starkly and so passionately. Balancing delicately between a hope for national regeneration and a frank acceptance of the harsh racial realities of antebellum America, Walker's *Appeal* strove finally—come what may—to point a way for African Americans to move toward greater integrity and freedom as individuals and as a people.

50. *Appeal*, 23, 62–65.
51. *Appeal*, 72–73.

"There is a great work for you to do": Circulating the *Appeal*

Walker only made the words of his pamphlet more terrifying to whites when he set about circulating it as widely as possible among the slaves in the South. Walker believed his pamphlet would be a critical wedge in helping the slaves understand their dignity, their significance to God, and their ability and duty to throw off their enslavement.

The rhetorical vigor of the *Appeal* derived in large part from its deep roots in African American oral culture, the culture to which the mass of African Americans—untutored and illiterate—were most indebted. Walker structured the work so that it was much more the inspired pronouncements of a black preacher filled with God and righteous anger against America's brutal racism than a closely reasoned and grammatically consistent treatise arguing coolly for the same point of view. Thus the aggressive, frenetic, and at times breathless volubility of the *Appeal*'s voice—a tenor regularly condemned by Walker's critics as evidence of his madness and marginality—was in fact carefully constructed to persuade by its vocal ardor and jarring images and to be readily accessible to the unlettered. Walker expected that the book would be read aloud to large groups of illiterate blacks far more often than read silently. Thus he warned educated and converted blacks: "Some of my brethren, who are sensible, do not take an interest in enlightening the minds of our more ignorant brethren respecting this BOOK, and in reading it to them, just as though they will not have either to stand or fall [i.e., before God] by what is written in this book."[52] Walker charged the educated and religious leaders among local black populations to read his *Appeal* to groups because their stature would lend immeasurable authority to its words.

> Men of colour, who are also of sense, for you particularly is my APPEAL designed. Our more ignorant brethren are not able to penetrate its value. I call upon you

52. *Appeal*, 74n.

therefore to cast your eyes upon the wretchedness of your brethren, and to do your utmost to enlighten them—*go to work and enlighten your brethren!*—Let the Lord see you doing what you can to rescue them and yourselves from degradation.[53]

The arrival of such a pamphlet in Southern towns and ports electrified white authorities.[54] When sixty copies were discovered to have been delivered by a white mariner to a black minister in Savannah, Georgia, in early December 1829, the town's mayor quickly alerted the governor and local authorities throughout the state. By month's end, new laws had been passed quarantining all black sailors entering Georgia ports and punishing severely anyone introducing seditious literature into the state. Nevertheless, a few weeks later, twenty copies were discovered with a white newspaper editor, Elijah Burritt, at the state capital in Milledgeville. At the same time, numerous copies were delivered by a free black courier to Richmond, Virginia, and circulated among local blacks. The governor was so alarmed that he immediately convened an extraordinary closed-door session of the General Assembly to reckon with the matter. In late March 1830, a number of copies were distributed to several black longshoremen in Charleston by another white seaman. The mariner was arrested, tried, and sentenced to one year of hard labor. In the same month, four blacks were arrested for circulating numerous copies in New Orleans. Two of them were slaves and two were free blacks, including a successful local shopkeeper named Robert Smith. By early 1830, the coastal South was in an uproar over the circulation of the *Appeal*, ever anxious about the scope of its penetration and the degree of its own subject population's excitement for it.

Yet the book's biggest inroads and disturbances were wrought in Walker's home turf of North Carolina. In August 1830 a Wilmington slave named Jacob Cowan had received two hundred copies from Walker with instructions to distrib-

53. *Appeal*, 30.
54. The following discussion of the *Appeal*'s circulation in the South is drawn from chapter 5 in Hinks, *To Awaken My Afflicted Brethren*, 116–72.

ute them throughout the state. Cowan's owner allowed him to keep a little tavern, which he then secretly used to circulate the *Appeal* until a free black alerted the town's authorities. By then, however, a local black Baptist preacher and a cooper had secured copies and were seen reading it, possibly to others. Whites in the town moved immediately to arrest the book's dissemination, and in the process killed the town's best black carpenter, sent the cooper to New York in chains, and sold Cowan deep into Alabama.

But that still did not end its circulation in the state. Later, in the fall of 1830, runaways along the coast were discovered with copies of the *Appeal,* and several indicated that a planned rising of some armed slaves near New Bern around Christmas was incited by it. Many of those slaves paid for it with their lives. By the end of the year, a North Carolina select committee concluded that "an extensive combination now exists" to incite the slaves to actions "subversive of good order" and blamed "the incendiary publication."[55]

Walker's *Appeal* never did ignite such a social conflagration. It did, however, strike real terror in authorities throughout the coastal South and spurred them to reinforce laws against slave literacy and the circulation of any inflammatory literature. Laws newly written in Wilmington and Savannah—modeled after one passed in Columbia, South Carolina, in 1822 after the failed Vesey conspiracy—required that any free black mariners from the North entering either of the ports be confined to jails during the term of their ship's presence there. This measure, they hoped, would eliminate contact and exchanges between Northern free blacks and local African Americans. Yet it accomplished this end more by driving many of the numerous blacks employed in the coastal carrying trade from working in it because they both reviled and feared these laws rather than by actually limiting the contact of those remaining in it with local blacks. Moreover, the cost of the incarceration was charged to the ship's captain and many chose to avoid the expense and inconvenience by hiring fewer black mariners.

---

55. Charles L. Coon, *The Beginnings of Public Education in North Carolina: A Documentary History, 1790–1840,* 2 vols. (Raleigh, N.C., 1908), 1:478.

Southern authorities were rightly concerned about the ability of Walker to place his pamphlet in the hands of those who were knowledgeable about the numerous covert communication systems existing among Southern slaves. They knew all too well that Southern blacks had used similar networks effectively during the conspiracies of Denmark Vesey and Gabriel. But Walker expanded on these local and regional applications and used the structures throughout the coastal South to deliver his message of black strength, dignity, freedom, and mission to as many slaves as possible. He envisioned a plan of black empowerment and mobilization that was the most sophisticated and extensive articulated in antebellum America. Walker's influence reverberated throughout antebellum America and beyond. Some contemporaries suggested that the evangelical *Appeal* helped spur Nat Turner to his bloody judgments in Southampton County, Virginia, in August 1831. This remains, however, only speculation.

David Walker and the Roots of American Abolitionism

Walker's impact on the dramatic rise of black political activism and of abolitionism by the late 1820s is even more evident. The *Appeal* declared that African Americans would no longer refrain from stating publicly and vividly what they had long said among themselves: it indicted white America for its brutality and hypocrisy and challenged all African Americans to submit no further. Nothing even vaguely resembling this vehement manifesto had ever been published before, and its boldness heralded a new and confident movement among blacks to end slavery and racial discrimination. Boston's Maria Stewart, one of the nation's leading black female abolitionists, revered Walker in the early 1830s as "the most noble, fearless, and undaunted" and as the one who had "distinguished himself [the most] in these modern days

by acting wholly in defence of African rights and liberty."[56]
Frederick Douglass readily recalled as late as 1883 that the
Appeal "startled the land like a trump of coming judgment"
and that David Walker "was before either Mr. [William
Lloyd] Garrison or Mr. [Benjamin] Lundy"—two of the most
eminent white abolitionists, both held dear by Douglass—in
inspiring the abolitionist movement and the defense of
black freedom and rights.[57] The Reverend Amos Beman, a
leading black abolitionist in antebellum Connecticut, recalled how his community would gather to hear the *Appeal*
"read and reread until [its] words were stamped in letters of
fire upon our soul."[58] Perhaps Henry Highland Garnet, the
great black orator and abolitionist, best summarized in 1848
the stature Walker attained for African Americans and all
who loathed slavery:

> Before the Anti-Slavery Reformation had assumed a
> form, he was ardently engaged in the work. His hands
> were always open to contribute to the wants of the fugi-
> tive. His house was the shelter and the home of the poor
> and needy. Mr. Walker is known principally by his "Ap-
> peal," but it was in his private walks, and by his unceas-
> ing labors in the cause of freedom, that he has made his
> memory sacred.[59]

Despite these testimonials, Walker's impact on the rise of
radical abolitionism, and especially on white abolitionists,
has usually been overlooked. This neglect has been due
largely to later historians' easy concurrence with Walker's

56. Maria Stewart, "An Address Delivered at the African Masonic Hall,"
in Marilyn Richardson, ed., *Maria W. Stewart, America's First Black Woman
Political Writer: Essays and Speeches* (Bloomington: Indiana University Press,
1987), 57.

57. Frederick Douglass, "Our Destiny Is Largely in Our Hands: An Address Delivered in Washington, D.C., on 16 April 1883," in John W. Blassin-
game and John R. McKivigan, eds., *The Frederick Douglass Papers*, 5 vols.
(New Haven: Yale University Press, 1992), 5:68–69.

58. Beman Papers, Scrapbook II, Beinecke Rare Book Library, Yale
University.

59. *Walker's APPEAL and Garnet's ADDRESS to the Slaves of the United
States of America* (Salem, N.H.: Ayer Company, 1989), vi.

relegation to a bloody and unstable political fringe by, for example, prominent abolitionist Benjamin Lundy. Lundy wrote in 1830 that the *Appeal* contained "the wildest strain of reckless fanaticism" and intended "to rouse the worst passions of human nature."[60] Even William Lloyd Garrison exclaimed in early 1831: "We deprecate the spirit and tendency of this Appeal." Yet he countered that the work held "many valuable truths and seasonable warnings."[61]

In fact, the *Appeal* powerfully influenced Garrison. As late as 1829, Garrison still supported the program of the American Colonization Society. The *Appeal* excoriated the hypocrisy and proslavery character of this plan. Walker's African American contemporary, William Watkins, wrote elegant condemnations of the ACS as well, but none was as extensive or as scathing as Walker's.[62] Watkins articulated the deep opposition of Northern free blacks to their removal and their mounting impatience with any argument counseling understanding for the situation of slaveholders and tolerance for a gradual end to slavery. When Garrison came to Boston in the spring of 1830 intending to start his new antislavery newspaper, *The Liberator,* he reached out especially to the city's black community, on whom he knew the viability of his newspaper depended. By then Garrison had become an ardent anticolonizationist and the most prominent proponent of the new and radical antislavery policy of immediatism. This new policy called for the immediate and unqualified abolition of slavery because slavery was a moral affront so huge that its perpetuation jeopardized the very existence of America and the salvation of its citizens. While many thinkers and forces influenced Garrison's transformation, the role of Walker was unquestionably paramount. It was no surprise that, despite his own criticism of the *Appeal* based on his pacifism, Garrison prominently and largely favorably covered Walker and his work in *The Liberator*'s first

60. *Genius of Universal Emancipation*, April 1830. Reprinted in the Appendix, Document IX, 107.

61. *The Liberator*, 8 January 1831.

62. See Bettye J. Gardner, ed., "Opposition to Emigration: A Selected Letter of William Watkins (The Colored Baltimorean)," *Journal of Negro History* 67 (Summer 1982), 155–58.

half-year. Garrison undoubtedly used this display to establish his understanding of and sympathy for the sensibilities
of the black community.

Tragically Walker was never to hear these accolades, to
witness the scale of his influence, or to share in the passion
for building the new antislavery movement in the early
1830s. On 6 August 1830, only a few days after his beloved
infant daughter, Lydia Ann, died of consumption, David
Walker too was carried away by the same dread disease,
which devastated urban environments during the summer
months. However, rumors that some secret Southern agent
had ushered Walker to death by violence or poison soon
emerged and flourished, despite confirmation of the cause
of death in his death record and the absence of any coro-
ner's report. In a brief 1848 biography of Walker, Henry
Highland Garnet acknowledged the rumors but was "not
prepared to affirm" them. More than likely, Walker died of
natural causes.

David Walker's journey ended at an anonymous gravesite
in section 13 of the South Boston cemetery, reserved for
blacks. But even as his body was lowered into the ground,
slaves were reading his book in the towns and swampy back-
waters of North Carolina and running his message up and
down the coast. Walker continued to traverse America, im-
ploring his afflicted brethren not to abandon their home-
land and to hold the nation to account for its ideals and
mission.

> I say unto you again, you must go to work and prepare
> the way of the Lord. There is a great work for you to
> do, as trifling as some of you may think of it. You have
> to prove to the Americans and the world, that we are
> MEN, and not *brutes*, as we have been represented, and
> by millions treated.[63]

63. *Appeal*, 32.

EDITOR'S NOTE:
THE THREE EDITIONS
OF THE *APPEAL*

Between the latter months of 1829 and probably sometime
in the spring of 1830, three different editions of David Walker's *Appeal* were published. Variations exist between these
three texts. The edition used in this volume is the third,
which incorporates all the changes made in the second edition as well as the final changes made for the third. The vast
majority of the alterations correct typographical errors or
reflect minor shifts in capitalization, spelling, and/or punc-
tuation. None of the variations finally alters the essential
message: that American slavery embodies one of the greatest
moral abominations in the history of the world, that blacks
must refuse to submit to slavery any longer, and that whites
must abolish it immediately if they are to avoid the swift,
certain, and terrifying judgment of God.

However, some of the more substantial variations in the
second and third editions amplified important components
of this message. Perhaps the most important amplification
concerned Walker's indictment of white American hypocrisy. Insertions in the second and third editions repeatedly
intensify this charge and subject their pretensions to greater
scornful ridicule. While in the first edition Walker refers
caustically to "the enlightened Americans," in the second
and third editions he emphasizes the phrase by placing it in
italics and recasting it as the *"enlightened Christians of
America."*[1] In the third edition, Walker makes a lengthy two-
page insertion that, among other things, further assails

---

1. David Walker, *Walker's Appeal, in Four Articles, Together With a Preamble
to the Colored Citizens of the World, But in Particular and Very Expressly to Those*

white American pretensions to Christianity and republicanism and warns that the true cruel character of Americans
will soon be exposed to the world: "God has however, very
recently published some of their secret crimes on the house
top, that the world may gaze on their Christianity and see of
what kind it is composed."[2] He reinforces this representation by highlighting particularly offensive discrimination
"by the white *Christians*" that has occurred since the first edition, such as the forced removal of a black man from Park
Street Church in Boston.[3] Later he mocked efforts to suppress his pamphlet: "Why, I thought the Americans proclaimed to the world that they are a happy, enlightened,
humane and Christian people, all the inhabitants of the
country enjoy equal Rights!! America is the asylum for the
oppressed of all nations."[4]

Some emendations also highlighted the special relationship of blacks to God and that the *Appeal* embodied divine
mandate. In a footnote at the end of Article I in the third
edition, Walker announced for the first time: "It is my solemn belief, that if ever the world becomes Christianized,
(which must certainly take place before long) it will be
through the means, under God of the *Blacks*."[5] By the second edition, Walker was chiding white America for imagin-
ing "that we wish to be white . . . but they are dreadfully
deceived—we wish to be just as it pleased our Creator to
have made us." In the same lengthy insert, he inquired:

*of the United States of America. Written in Boston, in the State of Massachusetts,
Sept. 28th, 1829* (Boston, 1829), 11; David Walker, *Walker's Appeal, in Four
Articles, Together With a Preamble, to the Colored Citizens of the World, But in
Particular, and Very Expressly to Those of the United States of America. Written in
Boston, in the State of Massachusetts, Sept. 28th, 1829*, second edition, with
corrections (Boston, 1830), 19; David Walker, *Walker's Appeal, in Four Arti-
cles; Together With a Preamble, to the Coloured Citizens of the World, But in Partic-
ular, and Very Expressly, to Those of the United States of America. Written in
Boston, State of Massachusetts, September 28, 1829*. Third and last edition, with
additional notes and corrections (Boston, 1830).

2. *Appeal*, 3rd ed., 55. (Here and hereafter all page references to the
third edition are to the present volume.)

3. *Appeal*, 3rd ed., 56.

4. *Appeal*, 3rd ed., 75n.

5. *Appeal*, 3rd ed., 20n.

"Why should we be afraid, when God is, and will continue (if we continue humble) to be on our side?"[6] Later in the same volume, he dismissed his detractors by linking his work directly to the intentions of God: "Do they believe that I would be so foolish as to put out a book of this kind, without strict—ah! very strict commandments of the Lord? . . . He will show you and the world, in due time, whether this book is for his glory, or written by me through envy to the whites, as some have represented."[7] Late in the third edition he reinforced this understanding: "I write without the fear of man, I am writing for my God."[8] These additions and others magnified God's special commitment to African Americans and the divine mission they had to fulfill. Walker's faith in this reality seems only to have deepened over the evolution of the three editions.

In the last two editions, Walker increased his attacks on the horrible defamation of black character leveled by whites. While this was certainly a central concern of his in the first edition as well, his assault intensifies in the latter two editions. In the second edition two footnotes are introduced in which Walker excoriated whites for characterizing African Americans "as a tribe of TALKING APES, void of *intellect!!! incapable* of LEARNING, &c." and for holding "us up with indignity as being incapable of acquiring knowledge!!!"[9] He also expanded his indictment of the cruel paradox that whites forced on blacks:

> See the inconsistency of the assertions of those wretches—they beat us inhumanly, sometimes almost to death, for attempting to inform ourselves, by reading the *Word* of our Maker, and at the same time tell us, that we are beings *void of intellect!!!!!* How admirably their practices agree with their professions in this case. Let me cry shame upon you Americans, for such outrages upon human nature!!![10]

6. *Appeal*, 2nd ed., 22–23.
7. *Appeal*, 2nd ed., 81–82n.
8. *Appeal*, 3rd ed., 56.
9. *Appeal*, 2nd ed., 72n, 73n.
10. *Appeal*, 2nd ed., 73n.

In a lengthy passage inserted in the third edition, Walker cataloged the brutalities and deprivations African Americans were subject to in antebellum America, all of which made self-improvement impossible as they fostered black demoralization. Yet the greatest cruelty they heaped on blacks was to then turn and designate them "an inferior race of beings! incapable of self-government!! . . . the meanest and laziest set of beings in the world . . . [who] are satisfied to rest in slavery to them [i.e., the whites] and their children!!!!!!"[11]

Walker also amplified his call to all blacks to begin assuming more responsibility for achieving their independence and dignity and not to wait quiescently for God or some hero to lead them. The most important examples of this are the two significant paragraphs inserted immediately before the Preamble in the third edition.[12] Walker summarized many key concerns in these compact paragraphs including a re-assertion of his belief that African Americans are "the most wretched, degraded and abject set of beings that ever lived since the world began." But arguably the most important is the final sentence in which he summons all African Americans to witness to their faith through ardent struggle against black degradation and enslavement.

> The day of our redemption from abject wretchedness draweth near, when we shall be enabled, in the most extended sense of the word, to stretch forth our hands to the LORD our GOD, but there must be a willingness on our part, for God to do these things for us, for we may be assured that he will not take us by the hairs of our head against our will and desire, and drag us from our very, mean, low and abject condition.

This passage evinces a postmillennial fervor—a faith that the Kingdom of God can be inaugurated on earth before the actual arrival of Jesus to reign—by the righteous activism of God's disciples. Walker's plea for mass demonstrations of

11. *Appeal*, 3rd ed., 68–69.
12. *Appeal*, 3rd ed., 2.

this faith is one of the foundations of the *Appeal*, and it is immeasurably strengthened by this call introduced in the final edition.

A further and no less important addition in this prefatory page is Walker's unrelenting expectation "that all coloured men, women and children, of every nation, language and tongue under heaven, will try to procure a copy of this Appeal and read it, or get someone to read it to them, for it is designed more particularly for them." At various points in the second and third editions, Walker calls on African Americans to obtain a copy of his pamphlet, understand it, and circulate it. In the second edition, as already noted, he declares the divine sanction for the book. He also continued to place special responsibility for disseminating the book on the shoulders of the better educated and politically awakened blacks: "Some of my brethren, who are sensible, do not take an interest in enlightening the minds of our more ignorant brethren respecting this BOOK, and in reading it to them, just as though they will not have either to stand or fall by what is written in this book."[13] By the third edition, he is not only summoning "my brethren [to] get my Book and read it," but also recounting as well the terror it has struck in Southern authorities by the might of its fearsome words.[14]

Finally, in the second and third editions Walker designates the English as unique white benefactors of blacks. This position is all but invisible in the first. In the second edition, Walker proclaimed:

> The English are the best friends the colored people have upon earth. Tho' they have oppressed us a little, and have colonies now in the West Indies, which oppress us *sorely*,—Yet notwithstanding they (the English) have done one hundred times more for the melioration of our condition, than all the other nations of the earth put together. The blacks cannot but respect the English as a nation, notwithstanding they have treated us a little

13. *Appeal*, 3rd ed., 74n.
14. *Appeal*, 3rd ed., 75n.

> cruel. . . . [T]hey are the greatest benefactors we have
> upon earth.

This position was reiterated in another insertion later in the
text.[15] This bold new assertion actually echoes similar praise
of English benefactors to blacks Walker made in an address
to the Massachusetts General Colored Association in December 1828.[16] Certainly Walker's enthusiasm for them is
informed by the legacy of Britain's leading role in ending
much of the Atlantic slave trade and by the mounting agitation in England then for abolishing slavery in their colonies,
a cause that would succeed by 1836. Nevertheless, there is
some irony in his statement because of England's continuing
connection with a brutal slavery in the West Indies, a reality
that Walker acknowledges in the passage but that he also
excoriates in the case of Jamaica in a footnote he inserts for
the first time in the third edition.[17] Clearly Walker continued
to the end with some lively ambivalence about England, and
it appears that he never fully resolved it for himself, except
perhaps by largely identifying the slavery of Jamaica exclusively with the white slaveholders on the island, not with the
English nation as a whole.

A few other insertions straddle several of the categories
outlined above. In the second edition, Walker appends an
insightful footnote on the etymology of the Latin word *Niger*,
presumably to establish its relationship to the American expletive "Nigger."[18] In a concise note, he explains that even
in Roman times the Latin word was used to refer to inanimate objects and animals that were black, which could be
owned and "which they considered inferior to the human
species." He argues that white Americans continue this understanding "by way of reproach for our colour." Walker
uses the word "Nigger" only once in the *Appeal*, and that in
the third edition only, using "Niger" on two occasions,
"Neger" once, and "Nigar" once in the third edition.[19] In

---

15. *Appeal*, 2nd ed., 53, 66.
16. This address is reprinted in the Appendix, Document II, 85–89.
17. *Appeal*, 3rd ed., 66n.
18. *Appeal*, 2nd ed., 65n.
19. *Appeal*, 1st ed., 11; *Appeal*, 2nd ed., 19; *Appeal*, 3rd ed., 11, 55.

fact, he seems to be equating at least "Neger," "Niger," and "Nigger," if not "Nigar" as well. In the first edition, Walker uses the word "Neger" on one occasion, but in the second edition that word is replaced by "Niger," the same word he used in the footnote mentioned above. Finally, in the third edition, Walker replaces that word with the term as traditionally construed, "Nigger." In each instance, Walker is deploying the word to highlight its role in designating people of African descent in America as supposedly inherently degraded and inferior, a perilous transformation in white American racial attitudes, which he argued was aggressively expanding by the late 1820s. There are indications by the 1820s the word was being used more commonly, and it certainly played a vital role in signifying the mounting designation of African Americans as a people uniquely degraded and wholly separate from and inferior to white Americans.[20]

As these insertions and the others reviewed above illustrate, Walker strove over the course of the three editions to be ever more forthright in displaying the full malignity of white America's subjugation of African Americans. This was the central function of all substantive textual variations over the three editions.

20. David Roediger discusses a few of the ways in which the word "Nigger" was used in antebellum America and the role it played in relegating all African Americans to the category of slave and innate degradation. See Roediger, *The Wages of Whiteness: Race and the Making of the American Working Class* (London: Verso, 1991), 108, 129–39, 144–45. While by no means definitive, *A Dictionary of American English on Historical Principles*, ed. Sir William A. Craigie and James R. Hulbert, 4 vols. (Chicago: University of Chicago Press, 1942), points to increased use of the expletive "Nigger" in the early decades of the nineteenth century, and the startling variety of phrases to which it and "Negro" were attached to suggest a host of negative connotations—degradation, inferiority, incompetence, coarseness, brute labor, shabbiness, stupidity, and much more. See ibid., 3:1589–92, 1601–3. I am also indebted to Patrick Rael of Bowdoin College for sharing with me some of his important research on African American identity in antebellum America, which included excellent examples of the increased use of the word "Nigger" in America by the 1820s. See "Why We Were Colored: The Names Controversy and African-American Identity in the Antebellum North," in Patrick Rael, *Colored Americans: Forging Black Protest in the Antebellum North* (Chapel Hill: University of North Carolina Press, forthcoming).

WALKER'S

APPEAL,

IN FOUR ARTICLES;

TOGETHER WITH

A PREAMBLE,

TO THE

COLOURED CITIZENS OF THE WORLD,

BUT IN PARTICULAR, AND VERY EXPRESSLY, TO THOSE OF

THE UNITED STATES OF AMERICA,

WRITTEN IN BOSTON, STATE OF MASSACHUSETTS,
SEPTEMBER 28, 1829.

THIRD AND LAST EDITION,
WITH ADDITIONAL NOTES, CORRECTIONS, &c.

Boston:
REVISED AND PUBLISHED BY DAVID WALKER.
....
1830.

☞ IT will be recollected, that I, in the first edition of my "Appeal," promised to demonstrate in the course of which, viz. in the course of my Appeal, to the satisfaction of the most incredulous mind, that we Coloured People of these United States, are, the most wretched, degraded and abject set of beings that ever lived since the world began, down to the present day, and, that, the white Christians of America, who hold us in slavery, (or, more properly speaking, pretenders to Christianity,) treat us more cruel and barbarous than any Heathen nation did any people whom it had subjected, or reduced to the same condition, that the Americans (who are, notwithstanding, looking for the Millennial day) have us. All I ask is, for a candid and careful perusal of this the third and last edition of my Appeal, where the world may see that we, the Blacks or Coloured People, are treated more cruel by the white Christians of America, than devils themselves ever treated a set of men, women and children on this earth. ☜

☞ It is expected that all coloured men, women and children,* of every nation, language and tongue under heaven, will try to procure a copy of this Appeal and read it, or get some one to read it to them, for it is designed more particularly for them. Let them remember, that though our cruel oppressors and murderers, may (if possible) treat us more cruel, as Pharaoh did the children of Israel,[1] yet the God of the Ethiopeans, has been pleased to hear our moans in consequence of oppression; and the day of our redemption from abject wretchedness draweth near, when we shall be enabled, in the most extended sense of the word, to stretch forth our hands to the LORD our GOD, but there must be a willingness on our part, for GOD to do these things for us, for we may be assured that he will not take us by the hairs of our head against our will and desire, and drag us from our very, mean, low and abject condition. ☜

*Who are not too deceitful, abject, and servile to resist the cruelties and murders inflicted upon us by the white slave holders, our enemies by nature.

PREAMBLE.

My dearly beloved Brethren and Fellow Citizens.

Having travelled over a considerable portion of these
United States, and having, in the course of my travels, taken
the most accurate observations of things as they exist—the
result of my observations has warranted the full and unshaken conviction, that we, (coloured people of these United
States,) are the most degraded, wretched, and abject set of
beings that ever lived since the world began; and I pray God
that none like us ever may live again until time shall be no
more. They tell us of the Israelites in Egypt,[2] the Helots in
Sparta,[3] and of the Roman Slaves,[4] which last were made up
from almost every nation under heaven, whose sufferings
under those ancient and heathen nations, were, in comparison with ours, under this enlightened and Christian nation,
no more than a cypher—or, in other words, those heathen
nations of antiquity, had but little more among them than
the name and form of slavery; while wretchedness and end-
less miseries were reserved, apparently in a phial, to be
poured out upon our fathers, ourselves and our children, by
Christian Americans!

These positions I shall endeavour, by the help of the
Lord, to demonstrate in the course of this *Appeal,* to the satisfaction of the most incredulous mind—and may God Al-

mighty, who is the Father of our Lord Jesus Christ, open your hearts to understand and believe the truth.

The *causes*, my brethren, which produce our wretchedness and miseries, are so very numerous and aggravating, that I believe the pen only of a Josephus[5] or a Plutarch,[6] can well enumerate and explain them. Upon subjects, then, of such incomprehensible magnitude, so impenetrable, and so notorious, I shall be obliged to omit a large class of, and content myself with giving you an exposition of a few of those, which do indeed rage to such an alarming pitch, that they cannot but be a perpetual source of terror and dismay to every reflecting mind.

I am fully aware, in making this appeal to my much afflicted and suffering brethren, that I shall not only be assailed by those whose greatest earthly desires are, to keep us in abject ignorance and wretchedness, and who are of the firm conviction that Heaven has designed us and our children to be slaves and *beasts of burden* to them and their children. I say, I do not only expect to be held up to the public as an ignorant, impudent and restless disturber of the public peace, by such avaricious creatures, as well as a mover of insubordination—and perhaps put in prison or to death, for giving a superficial exposition of our miseries, and exposing tyrants. But I am persuaded, that many of my brethren, particularly those who are ignorantly in league with slaveholders or tyrants, who acquire their daily bread by the blood and sweat of their more ignorant brethren—and not a few of those too, who are too ignorant to see an inch beyond their noses, will rise up and call me cursed—Yea, the jealous ones among us will perhaps use more abject subtlety, by affirming that this work is not worth perusing, that we are well situated, and there is no use in trying to better our condition, for we cannot. I will ask one question here.—Can our condition be any worse?—Can it be more mean and abject? If there are any changes, will they not be for the better, though they may appear for the worst at first? Can they get us any lower? Where can they get us? They are afraid to treat us worse, for they know well, the day they do it they are gone. But against all accusations which may or can be preferred against me, I appeal to Heaven for my motive in writing—who knows that my object is, if possible, to awaken in the breasts of my afflicted, degraded and slumbering brethren, a spirit of inquiry and investigation respecting our miseries and wretchedness in this *Republican Land of Liberty!!!!!!*

The sources from which our miseries are derived, and on which I shall comment, I shall not combine in one, but shall put them under distinct heads and expose them in their turn; in doing which, keeping truth on my side, and not departing from the strictest rules of morality, I shall endeavour to penetrate, search out, and lay them open for your inspection. If you cannot or will not profit by them, I shall have done *my* duty to you, my country and my God.

And as the inhuman system of *slavery,* is the *source* from which most of our miseries proceed, I shall begin with that *curse to nations,* which has spread terror and devastation through so many nations of antiquity, and which is raging to such a pitch at the present day in Spain and in Portugal.[7] It had one tug in England, in France, and in the United States of America; yet the inhabitants thereof, do not learn wisdom, and erase it entirely from their dwellings and from all with whom they have to do. The fact is, the labour of slaves comes so cheap to the avaricious usurpers, and is (as they think) of such great utility to the country where it exists, that those who are actutated by sordid avarice only, overlook the evils, which will as sure as the Lord lives, follow after the good. In fact, they are so happy to keep in ignorance and degradation, and to receive the homage and the labour of the slaves, they forget that God rules in the armies of heaven and among the inhabitants of the earth, having his ears continually open to the cries, tears and groans of his oppressed people; and being a just and holy Being will at one day appear fully in behalf of the oppressed, and arrest the progress of the avaricious oppressors; for although the destruction of the oppressors God may not effect by the oppressed, yet the Lord our God will bring other destructions upon them—for not unfrequently will he cause them to rise up one against another, to be split and divided, and to oppress each other, and sometimes to open hostilities with sword in hand. Some may ask, what is the matter with this united and happy people?—Some say it is the cause of political usurpers, tyrants,

oppressors, &c. But has not the Lord an oppressed and suffering people among them? Does the Lord condescend to
hear their cries and see their tears in consequence of oppression? Will he let the oppressors rest comfortably and happy
always? Will he not cause the very children of the oppressors
to rise up against them, and oftimes put them to death?
"God works in many ways his wonders to perform."

I will not here speak of the destructions which the Lord
brought upon Egypt, in consequence of the oppression and
consequent groans of the oppressed—of the hundreds and
thousands of Egyptians whom God hurled into the Red Sea
for afflicting his people in their land[8]—of the Lord's suffering people in Sparta or Lacedaemon,[9] the land of the truly
famous Lycurgus[10]—nor have I time to comment upon the
cause which produced the fierceness with which Sylla
usurped the title, and absolutely acted as dictator of the
Roman people[11]—the conspiracy of Cataline[12]—the conspiracy against, and murder of Caesar in the Senate house[13]—
the spirit with which Marc Antony made himself master of
the commonwealth[14]—his associating Octavius and Lipidus
with himself in power—their dividing the provinces of Rome
among themselves[15]—their attack and defeat, on the plains
of Phillipi,[16] of the last defenders of their liberty, (Brutus
and Cassius)[17]—the tyranny of Tiberius,[18] and from him to
the final overthrow of Constantinople by the Turkish Sultan,
Mahomed II. A.D. 1453.[19] I say, I shall not take up time to
speak of the *causes* which produced so much wretchedness
and massacre among those heathen nations, for I am aware
that you know too well, that God is just, as well as merciful!—I shall call your attention a few moments to that *Christian* nation, the Spaniards—while I shall leave almost
unnoticed, that avaricious and cruel people, the Portuguese,
among whom all true hearted Christians and lovers of Jesus
Christ, must evidently see the judgments of God displayed.
To show the judgments of God upon the Spaniards, I shall
occupy but a little time, leaving a plenty of room for the
candid and unprejudiced to reflect.

All persons who are acquainted with history, and particularly the Bible, who are not blinded by the God of this world,
and are not actuated solely by avarice—who are able to lay

aside prejudice long enough to view candidly and impartially, things as they were, are, and probably will be—who are willing to admit that God made man to serve Him *alone*, and that man should have no other Lord or Lords but Himself—that God Almighty is the *sole proprietor* or *master* of the WHOLE human family, and will not on any consideration admit of a colleague, being unwilling to divide his glory with another—and who can dispense with prejudice long enough to admit that we are *men*, notwithstanding our *improminent noses* and *woolly heads,* and believe that we feel for our fathers, mothers, wives and children, as well as the whites do for theirs.—I say, all who are permitted to see and believe these things, can easily recognize the judgments of God among the Spaniards. Though others may lay the cause of the fierceness with which they cut each other's throats, to some other circumstance, yet they who believe that God is a God of justice, will believe that SLAVERY *is the principal cause.*

While the Spaniards are running about upon the field of battle cutting each other's throats, has not the Lord an afflicted and suffering people in the midst of them, whose cries and groans in consequence of oppression are continually pouring into the ears of the God of justice? Would they not cease to cut each other's throats, if they could? But how can they? The very support which they draw from government to aid them in perpetrating such enormities, does it not arise in a great degree from the wretched victims of oppression among them? And yet they are calling for *Peace!—Peace!!* Will any peace be given unto them? Their destruction may indeed be procrastinated awhile, but can it continue long, while they are oppressing the Lord's people? Has He not the hearts of all men in His hand? Will he suffer one part of his creatures to go on oppressing another like brutes always, with impunity? And yet, those avaricious wretches are calling for *Peace!!!!* I declare, it does appear to me, as though some nations think God is asleep, or that he made the Africans for nothing else but to dig their mines and work their farms, or they cannot believe history, sacred or profane. I ask every man who has a heart, and is blessed with the privilege of believing—Is not God a God of justice to *all* his creatures? Do you say he is? Then if he gives peace and tranquillity to tyrants, and permits them to keep our fathers, our mothers, ourselves and our children in eternal ignorance and wretchedness, to support them and their families, would he be to us a God of *justice?* I ask, O ye *Christians!!!* who hold us and our children in the most abject ignorance and degradation, that ever a people were afflicted with since the world began—I say, if God gives you peace and tranquillity, and suffers you thus to go on afflicting us, and our children, who have never given you the least provocation— would he be to us *a God of justice?* If you will allow that we are MEN, who feel for each other, does not the blood of our fathers and of us their children, cry aloud to the Lord of Sabaoth against you, for the cruelties and murders with which you have, and do continue to afflict us. But it is time for me to close my remarks on the suburbs, just to enter more fully into the interior of this system of cruelty and oppression.

ARTICLE I.

OUR WRETCHEDNESS IN CONSEQUENCE OF SLAVERY.

My beloved brethren:—The Indians of North and of South America[20]—the Greeks[21]—the Irish, subjected under the king of Great Britain[22]—the Jews, that ancient people of the Lord[23]—the inhabitants of the islands of the sea[24]—in fine, all the inhabitants of the earth, (except however, the sons of Africa) are called *men,* and of course are, and ought to be free. But we, (coloured people) and our children are *brutes!!* and of course are, and *ought to be* SLAVES to the American people and their children forever!! to dig their mines and work their farms; and thus go on enriching them, from one generation to another with our *blood* and our *tears!!!!*

I promised in a preceding page to demonstrate to the satisfaction of the most incredulous, that we, (coloured people of these United States of America) are the *most wretched, degraded* and *abject* set of beings that *ever lived* since the world began, and that the white Americans having reduced us to the wretched state of *slavery,* treat us in that condition *more cruel* (they being an enlightened and Christian people,) than any heathen nation did any people whom it had reduced to our condition. These affirmations are so well confirmed in the minds of all unprejudiced men, who have taken the trouble to read histories, that they need no elucidation from me. But to put them beyond all doubt, I refer you in the first place to the children of Jacob,[25] or of Israel in Egypt, under

Pharaoh and his people. Some of my brethren do not know who Pharaoh and the Egyptians were—I know it to be a fact, that some of them take the Egyptians to have been a gang of *devils,* not knowing any better, and that they (Egyptians) having got possession of the Lord's people, treated them *nearly* as cruel as *Christian Americans* do us, at the present day. For the information of such, I would only mention that the Egyptians, were Africans or coloured people, such as we are—some of them yellow and others dark—a mixture of Ethiopians and the natives of Egypt—about the same as you see the coloured people of the United States at the present day.—I say, I call your attention then, to the children of Jacob, while I point out particularly to you his son Joseph,[26] among the rest, in Egypt.

"And Pharaoh, said unto Joseph, . . . thou shalt be over my house, and according unto thy word shall all my people be ruled: only in the throne will I be greater than thou.*

"And Pharaoh said unto Joseph, see, I have set thee over all the land of Egypt."†

"And Pharaoh said unto Joseph, I am Pharaoh, and without thee shall no man lift up his hand or foot in all the land of Egypt."‡

Now I appeal to heaven and to earth, and particularly to the American people themselves, who cease not to declare that our condition is not *hard,* and that we are comparatively satisfied to rest in wretchedness and misery, under them and their children. Not, indeed, to show me a coloured President, a Governor, a Legislator, a Senator, a Mayor, or an Attorney at the Bar.—But to show me a man of colour, who holds the low office of Constable, or one who sits in a Juror Box, even on a case of one of his wretched brethren, throughout this great Republic!![27]—But let us pass Joseph the son of Israel a little farther in review, as he existed with that heathen nation.

"And Pharaoh called Joseph's name Zaphnathpaaneah; and he gave him to wife Asenath the daughter of Potipherah

---

*See Genesis, chap. xli. [39–40].

†[xli. 41.]

[‡] xli. 44.

priest of On. And Joseph went out over all the land of Egypt."*

Compare the above, with the American institutions. Do they not institute laws to prohibit us from marrying among the whites?[28] I would wish, candidly, however, before the Lord, to be understood, that I would not give a *pinch of snuff* to be married to any white person I ever saw in all the days of my life. And I do say it, that the black man, or man of colour, who will leave his own colour (provided he can get one, who is good for any thing) and marry a white woman, to be a double slave to her, just because she is *white*, ought to be treated by her as he surely will be, viz: as a NIGGER!!!! It is not, indeed, what I care about inter-marriages with the whites, which induced me to pass this subject in review; for the Lord knows, that there is a day coming when they will be glad enough to get into the company of the blacks, notwithstanding, we are, in this generation, levelled by them, almost on a level with the brute creation: and some of us they treat even worse than they do the brutes that perish. I only made this extract to show how much lower we are held, and how much more cruel we are treated by the Americans, than were the children of Jacob, by the Egyptians.—We will notice the sufferings of Israel some further, under *heathen Pharaoh*, compared with ours under the *enlightened Christians of America.*

"And Pharaoh spoke unto Joseph, saying, thy father and thy brethren are come unto thee:

"The land of Egypt is before thee: in the best of the land make thy father and brethren to dwell; in the land of Goshen let them dwell: and if thou knowest any men of activity among them, then make them rulers over my cattle."†

I ask those people who treat us so *well*, Oh! I ask them, where is the most barren spot of land which they have given unto us? Israel had the most fertile land in all Egypt. Need I mention the very notorious fact, that I have known a poor man of colour, who laboured night and day, to acquire a little money, and having acquired it, he vested it in a small

*xli. 45.
†Genesis, chap. xlvii. 5, 6.

piece of land, and got him a house erected thereon, and having paid for the whole, he moved his family into it, where he was suffered to remain but nine months, when he was cheated out of his property by a white man, and driven out of door! And is not this the case generally? Can a man of colour buy a piece of land and keep it peaceably? Will not some white man try to get it from him, even if it is in a *mud hole?* I need not comment any farther on a subject, which all, both black and white, will readily admit. But I must, really, observe that in this very city, when a man of colour dies, if he owned any real estate it most generally falls into the hands of some white person. The wife and children of the deceased may weep and lament if they please, but the estate will be kept snug enough by its white possessor.

But to prove farther that the condition of the Israelites was better under the Egyptians than ours is under the whites. I call upon the professing Christians, I call upon the philanthropist, I call upon the very tyrant himself, to show me a page of history, either sacred or profane, on which a verse can be found, which maintains, that the Egyptians heaped the *insupportable insult* upon the children of Israel, by telling them that they were not of the *human family.* Can the whites deny this charge? Have they not, after having reduced us to the deplorable condition of slaves under their feet, held us up as descending originally from the tribes of *Monkeys* or *Orang-Outangs?* O! my God! I appeal to every man of feeling—is not this insupportable? Is it not heaping the most gross insult upon our miseries, because they have got us under their feet and we cannot help ourselves? Oh! pity us we pray thee, Lord Jesus, Master.—Has Mr. Jefferson declared to the world, that we are inferior to the whites, both in the endowments of our bodies and our minds?[29] It is indeed surprising, that a man of such great learning, combined with such excellent natural parts, should speak so of a set of men in chains. I do not know what to compare it to, unless, like putting one wild deer in an iron cage, where it will be secured, and hold another by the side of the same, then let it go, and expect the one in the cage to run as fast as the one at liberty. So far, my brethren, were the Egyptians from heaping these insults upon their slaves, that Pharaoh's daughter took Moses,[30] a son of Israel for her own, as will appear by the following.

"And Pharaoh's daughter said unto her, [Moses' mother] take this child away, and nurse it for me, and I will pay thee thy wages. And the woman took the child [Moses] and nursed it.

"And the child grew, and she brought him unto Pharaoh's daughter and he became her son. And she called his name Moses: and she said because I drew him out of the water."*

In all probability, Moses would have become Prince Regent to the throne, and no doubt, in process of time but he would have been seated on the throne of Egypt. But he had rather suffer shame, with the people of God, than to enjoy pleasures with that wicked people for a season. O! that the coloured people were long since of Moses' excellent disposition, instead of courting favour with, and telling news and lies to our *natural enemies,* against each other—aiding them to keep their hellish chains of slavery upon us. Would we not long before this time, have been respectable men, instead of such wretched victims of oppression as we are? Would they be able to drag our mothers, our fathers, our wives, our children and ourselves, around the world in chains and handcuffs as they do, to dig up gold and silver for them and theirs? This question, my brethren, I leave for you to digest; and may God Almighty force it home to your hearts. Remember that unless you are united, keeping your tongues within your teeth, you will be afraid to trust your secrets to each other, and thus perpetuate our miseries under the *Christians!!!!*

☞ADDITION.—Remember, also to lay humble at the feet of our Lord and Master Jesus Christ, with prayers and fastings. Let our enemies go on with their butcheries, and at once fill up their cup. Never make an attempt to gain our freedom or *natural right,* from under our cruel oppressors and murderers, until you see your way clear†—when that

*See Exodus, chap. ii, 9, 10.

†It is not to be understood here, that I mean for us to wait until God shall take us by the hair of our heads and drag us out of abject wretchedness and slavery, nor do I mean to convey the idea for us to wait until our enemies shall make preparations, and call us to seize those preparations, take

hour arrives and you move, be not afraid or dismayed; for be you assured that Jesus Christ the King of heaven and of earth who is the God of justice and of armies, will surely go before you. And those enemies who have for hundreds of years stolen our *rights,* and kept us ignorant of Him and His divine worship, he will remove. Millions of whom, are this day, so ignorant and avaricious, that they cannot conceive how God can have an attribute of justice, and show mercy to us because it pleased Him to make us black—which colour, Mr. Jefferson calls unfortunate!!!!!! As though we are not as thankful to our God, for having made us as it pleased himself, as they, (the whites,) are for having made them white. They think because they hold us in their infernal chains of slavery, that we wish to be white, or of their color—but they are dreadfully deceived—we wish to be just as it pleased our Creator to have made us, and no avaricious and unmerciful wretches, have any business to make slaves of, or hold us in slavery. How would they like for us to make slaves of, and hold them in cruel slavery, and murder them as they do us?—But is Mr. Jefferson's assertions true? viz. "that it is unfortunate for us that our Creator has been pleased to make us *black.*" We will not take his say so, for the fact. The world will have an opportunity to see whether it is unfortunate for us, that our Creator *has made us* darker than the *whites.*

Fear not the number and education of our *enemies,* against whom we shall have to contend for our lawful right; guaranteed to us by our Maker; for why should we be afraid, when God is, and will continue, (if we continue humble) to be on our side?

The man who would not fight under our Lord and Master Jesus Christ, in the glorious and heavenly cause of freedom and of God—to be delivered from the most wretched, abject and servile slavery, that ever a people was afflicted with since

---

it away from them, and put every thing before us to death, in order to gain our freedom which God has given us. For you must remember that we are men as well as they. God has been pleased to give us two eyes, two hands, two feet, and some sense in our heads as well as they. They have no more right to hold us in slavery than we have to hold them, we have just as much right, in the sight of God, to hold them and their children in slavery and wretchedness, as they have to hold us, and no more.

the foundation of the world, to the present day—ought to be kept with all of his children or family, in slavery, or in chains, to be butchered by his *cruel enemies.* ◄◄

I saw a paragraph, a few years since, in a South Carolina paper, which, speaking of the barbarity of the Turks, it said: "The Turks are the most barbarous people in the world— they treat the Greeks more like *brutes* than human beings."[31] And in the same paper was an advertisement, which said: "Eight well built Virginia and Maryland *Negro fellows* and four *wenches* will positively be *sold* this day, *to the highest bidder!*" And what astonished me still more was, to see in this same *humane* paper!! the cuts of three men, with clubs and budgets on their backs, and an advertisement offering a considerable sum of money for their apprehension and delivery. I declare, it is really so amusing to hear the Southerners and Westerners of this country talk about *barbarity,* that it is positively, enough to make a man *smile.*

The sufferings of the Helots among the Spartans,[32] were somewhat severe, it is true, but to say that theirs, were as severe as ours among the Americans, I do most strenuously deny—for instance, can any man show me an article on a page of ancient history which specifies, that, the Spartans chained, and handcuffed the Helots, and dragged them from their wives and children, children from their parents, mothers from their suckling babes, wives from their husbands, driving them from one end of the country to the other? Notice the Spartans were heathens, who lived long before our Divine Master made his appearance in the flesh. Can Christian Americans deny these barbarous cruelties? Have you not, Americans, having subjected us under you, added to these miseries, by insulting us in telling us to our face, because we are helpless, that we are not of the human family? I ask you, O! Americans, I ask you, in the name of the Lord, can you deny these charges? Some perhaps may deny, by saying, that they never thought or said that we were not men. But do not actions speak louder than words?— have they not made provisions for the Greeks, and Irish? Nations who have never done the least thing for them, while *we,* who have enriched their country with our blood and tears—have dug up gold and silver for them and their children, from generation to generation, and are in more miseries than any other people under heaven, are not seen, but by comparatively, a handful of the American people? There are indeed, more ways to kill a dog, besides choking it to death with butter. Further—The Spartans or Lacedaemonians, had some frivolous pretext, for enslaving the Helots, for they (Helots) while being free inhabitants of Sparta, stirred up an intestine commotion, and were, by the Spartans subdued, and made prisoners of war. Consequently, they and their children were condemned to perpetual slavery.*

I have been for years troubling the pages of historians, to find out what our fathers have done to the *white Christians of America*, to merit such condign punishment as they have inflicted on them, and do continue to inflict on us their children. But I must aver, that my researches have hitherto been to no effect. I have therefore, come to the immoveable conclusion, that they (Americans) have, and do continue to punish us for nothing else, but for enriching them and their country. For I cannot conceive of anything else. Nor will I ever believe otherwise, until the Lord shall convince me.

The world knows, that slavery as it existed among the Romans, (which was the primary cause of their destruction) was, comparatively speaking, no more than a *cypher*, when compared with ours under the Americans. Indeed I should not have noticed the Roman slaves, had not the very learned and penetrating Mr. Jefferson said, "when a master was murdered, all his slaves in the same house, or within hearing, were condemned to death."†[33]—Here let me ask Mr. Jefferson, (but he is gone to answer at the bar of God, for the deeds done in his body while living,) I therefore ask the whole American people, had I not rather die, or be put to death, than to be a slave to any tyrant, who takes not only my own, but my wife and children's lives by the inches? Yea, would I meet death with avidity far! far!! in preference to such *servile submission* to the murderous hands of tyrants. Mr. Jefferson's very severe remarks on us have been so exten-

---

*See Dr. Goldsmith's History of Greece[34]—page 9. See also, Plutarch's Lives. The Helots subdued by Agis, king of *Sparta*.[35]

†See his Notes on Virginia, page 210.

sively argued upon by men whose attainments in literature, I shall never be able to reach, that I would not have meddled with it, were it not to solicit each of my brethren, who has the spirit of a man, to buy a copy of Mr. Jefferson's "Notes on Virginia," and put it in the hand of his son. For let no one of us suppose that the refutations which have been written by our white friends are enough—they are *whites*—we are *blacks*. We, and the world wish to see the charges of Mr. Jefferson refuted by the blacks *themselves*, according to their chance; for we must remember that what the whites have written respecting this subject, is other men's labours, and did not emanate from the blacks. I know well, that there are some talents and learning among the coloured people of this country, which we have not a chance to develope, in consequence of oppression; but our oppression ought not to hinder us from acquiring all we can. For we will have a chance to develope them by and by. God will not suffer us, always to be oppressed. Our sufferings will come to an *end*, in spite of all the Americans this side of *eternity*. Then we will want all the learning and talents among ourselves, and perhaps more, to govern ourselves.—"Every dog must have its day," the American's is coming to an end.

But let us review Mr. Jefferson's remarks respecting us some further. Comparing our miserable fathers, with the learned philosophers of Greece, he says: "Yet notwithstanding these and other discouraging circumstances among the Romans, their slaves were often their rarest artists. They excelled too, in science, insomuch as to be usually employed as tutors to their master's children; Epictetus, Terence and Phædrus, were slaves,—but they were of the race of whites. It is not their *condition* then, but *nature*, which has produced the distinction."*[36] See this, my brethren!! Do you believe that this assertion is swallowed by millions of the whites? Do you know that Mr. Jefferson was one of as great characters as ever lived among the whites? See his writings for the world, and public labours for the United States of America. Do you believe that the assertions of such a man, will pass away into oblivion unobserved by this people and the world?

---

*See his Notes on Virginia, page 211.

If you do you are much mistaken—See how the American people treat us—have we souls in our bodies? Are we men who have any spirits at all? I know that there are many *swell-bellied* fellows among us, whose greatest object is to fill their stomachs. Such I do not mean—I am after those who know and feel, that we are MEN, as well as other people; to them, I say, that unless we try to refute Mr. Jefferson's arguments respecting us, we will only establish them.

But the slaves among the Romans. Every body who has read history, knows, that as soon as a slave among the Romans obtained his freedom, he could rise to the greatest eminence in the State, and there was no law instituted to hinder a slave from buying his freedom. Have not the Americans instituted laws to hinder us from obtaining our freedom? Do any deny this charge? Read the laws of Virginia, North Carolina, &c.[37] Further: have not the Americans instituted laws to prohibit a man of colour from obtaining and holding any office whatever, under the government of the United States of America? Now, Mr. Jefferson tells us, that our condition is not so hard, as the slaves were under the Romans!!!!!!

It is time for me to bring this article to a close. But before I close it, I must observe to my brethren that at the close of the first Revolution in this country, with Great Britain, there were but thirteen States in the Union, now there are twenty-four,[38] most of which are slave-holding States, and the whites are dragging us around in chains and in handcuffs, to their new States and Territories to work their mines and farms, to enrich them and their children—and millions of them believing firmly that we being a little darker than they, were made by our Creator to be an inheritance to them and their children for ever—the same as a parcel of *brutes.*

Are we MEN!!—I ask you, O my brethren! are we MEN? Did our Creator make us to be slaves to dust and ashes like ourselves? Are they not dying worms as well as we? Have they not to make their appearance before the tribunal of Heaven, to answer for the deeds done in the body, as well as we? Have we any other Master but Jesus Christ alone? Is he not their Master as well as ours?—What right then, have we to obey and call any other Master, but Himself? How we could be so *submissive* to a gang of men, whom we cannot tell whether they are *as good* as ourselves or not, I never could conceive. However, this is shut up with the Lord, and we cannot precisely tell—but I declare, we judge men by their works.

The whites have always been an unjust, jealous, unmerciful, avaricious and blood-thirsty set of beings, always seeking after power and authority.—We view them all over the confederacy of Greece, where they were first known to be any thing, (in consequence of education) we see them there, cutting each other's throats—trying to subject each other to wretchedness and misery—to effect which, they used all kinds of deceitful, unfair, and unmerciful means. We view them next in Rome, where the spirit of tyranny and deceit raged still higher. We view them in Gaul, Spain, and in Britain.—In fine, we view them all over Europe, together with what were scattered about in Asia and Africa, as heathens, and we see them acting more like devils than accountable men. But some may ask, did not the blacks of Africa, and the mulattoes of Asia,[39] go on in the same way as did the whites of Europe. I answer, no—they never were half so avaricious, deceitful and unmerciful as the whites, according to their knowledge.

But we will leave the whites or Europeans as heathens, and take a view of them as Christians, in which capacity we see them as cruel, if not more so than ever. In fact, take them as a body, they are ten times more cruel, avaricious and unmerciful than ever they were; for while they were heathens, they were bad enough it is true, but it is positively a fact that they were not quite so audacious as to go and take vessel loads of men, women and children, and in cold blood, and through devilishness, throw them into the sea, and murder them in all kind of ways. While they were heathens, they were too ignorant for such barbarity. But being Christians, enlighted and sensible, they are completely prepared for such hellish cruelties. Now suppose God were to give them more sense, what would they do? If it were possible, would they not *dethrone* Jehovah and seat themselves upon his throne? I therefore, in the name and fear of the Lord God of Heaven and of earth, divested of prejudice either on the

side of my colour or that of the whites, advance my suspicion
of them, whether they are *as good by nature* as we are or not.
Their actions, since they were known as a people, have been
the reverse, I do indeed suspect them, but this, as I before
observed, is shut up with the Lord, we cannot exactly tell, it
will be proved in succeeding generations.—The whites have
had the essence of the gospel as it was preached by my master and his apostles—the Ethiopians have not, who are to
have it in its meridian splendor—the Lord will give it to
them to their satisfaction. I hope and pray my God, that they
will make good use of it, that it may be well with them.*

---

*It is my solemn belief, that if ever the world becomes Christianized,
(which must certainly take place before long) it will be through the means,
under God of the *Blacks*, who are now held in wretchedness, and degradation, by the white *Christians* of the world, who before they learn to do justice
to us before our Maker—and be reconciled to us, and reconcile us to them,
and by that means have clear consciences before God and man.—Send out
Missionaries to convert the Heathens, many of whom after they cease to
worship gods, which neither see nor hear, become ten times more the children of Hell, then ever they were, why what is the reason? Why the reason
is obvious, they must learn to do justice at home, before they go into distant
lands, to display their charity, Christianity, and benevolence; when they
learn to do justice, God will accept their offering, (no man may think that I
am against Missionaries for I am not, my object is to see justice done at
home, before we go to convert the Heathens.)[40]

ARTICLE II.

OUR WRETCHEDNESS IN CONSEQUENCE OF IGNORANCE.

Ignorance, my brethren, is a mist, low down into the very dark and almost impenetrable abyss in which, our fathers for many centuries have been plunged. The Christians, and enlightened of Europe, and some of Asia, seeing the ignorance and consequent degradation of our fathers, instead of trying to enlighten them, by teaching them that religion and light with which God had blessed them, they have plunged them into wretchedness ten thousand times more intolerable, than if they had left them entirely to the Lord, and to add to their miseries, deep down into which they have plunged them tell them, that they are an *inferior* and *distinct race* of beings, which they will be glad enough to recall and swallow by and by. Fortune and misfortune, two inseparable companions, lay rolled up in the wheel of events, which have from the creation of the world, and will continue to take place among men until God shall dash worlds together.

When we take a retrospective view of the arts and sciences—the wise legislators—the Pyramids, and other magnificent buildings—the turning of the channel of the river Nile,[41] by the sons of Africa or of Ham, among whom learning originated,[42] and was carried thence into Greece, where it was improved upon and refined. Thence among the Romans, and all over the then enlightened parts of the world, and it has been enlightening the dark and benighted minds

of men from then, down to this day. I say, when I view retro-
spectively, the renown of that once mighty people, the children of our great progenitor I am indeed cheered. Yea
further, when I view that mighty son of Africa, HANNIBAL,
one of the greatest generals of antiquity, who defeated and
cut off so many thousands of the white Romans or murderers, and who carried his victorious arms, to the very gate of
Rome, and I give it as my candid opinion, that had Carthage
been well united and had given him good support, he would
have carried that cruel and barbarous city by storm.[43] But
they were dis-united, as the coloured people are now, in the
United States of America, the reason our natural enemies
are enabled to keep their feet on our throats.

Beloved brethren—here let me tell you, and believe it,
that the Lord our God, as true as he sits on his throne in
heaven, and as true as our Saviour died to redeem the world,
will give you a Hannibal, and when the Lord shall have
raised him up, and given him to you for your possession, O
my suffering brethren! remember the divisions and consequent sufferings of *Carthage* and of *Hayti*.[44] Read the history
particularly of Hayti, and see how they were butchered by
the whites, and do you take warning. The person whom God
shall give you, give him your support and let him go his
length, and behold in him the salvation of your God. God
will indeed, deliver you through him from your deplorable
and wretched condition under the Christians of America. I
charge you this day before my God to lay no obstacle in his
way, but let him go.

The whites want slaves, and want us for their slaves, but
some of them will curse the day they ever saw us. As true as
the sun ever shone in its meridian splendor, my colour will
root some of them out of the very face of the earth. They
shall have enough of making slaves of, and butchering, and
murdering us in the manner which they have. No doubt
some may say that I write with a bad spirit, and that I being
a black, wish these things to occur. Whether I write with a
bad or a good spirit, I say if these things do not occur in
their proper time, it is because the world in which we live
does not exist, and we are deceived with regard to its existence.—It is immaterial however to me, who believe, or who

refuse—though I should like to see the whites repent peradventure God may have mercy on them, some however, have gone so far that their cup must be filled.

But what need have I to refer to antiquity, when Hayti, the glory of the blacks and terror of tyrants, is enough to convince the most avaricious and stupid of wretches—which is at this time, and I am sorry to say it, plagued with that scourge of nations, the Catholic religion; but I hope and pray God that she may yet rid herself of it, and adopt in its stead the Protestant faith; also, I hope that she may keep peace within her borders and be united, keeping a strict look out for tyrants, for if they get the least chance to injure her, they will avail themselves of it, as true as the Lord lives in heaven. But one thing which gives me joy is, that they are men who would be cut off to a man, before they would yield to the combined forces of the whole world—in fact, if the whole world was combined against them, it could not do any thing with them, unless the Lord delivers them up.

Ignorance and treachery one against the other—a grovelling servile and abject submission to the lash of tyrants, we see plainly, my brethren, are not the natural elements of the blacks, as the Americans try to make us believe; but these are misfortunes which God has suffered our fathers to be enveloped in for many ages, no doubt in consequence of their disobedience to their Maker, and which do, indeed, reign at this time among us, almost to the destruction of all other principles: for I must truly say, that ignorance, the mother of treachery and deceit, gnaws into our very vitals. Ignorance, as it now exists among us, produces a state of things, Oh my Lord! too horrible to present to the world. Any man who is curious to see the full force of ignorance developed among the coloured people of the United States of America, has only to go into the southern and western states of this confederacy, where, if he is not a tyrant, but has the feelings of a human being, who can feel for a fellow creature, he may see enough to make his very heart bleed! He may see there, a son take his mother, who bore almost the pains of death to give him birth, and by the command of a tyrant, strip her as naked as she came into the world, and apply the cow-hide to her, until she falls a victim to death in the road! He may see a husband take his dear wife, not unfrequently in a pregnant state, and perhaps far advanced, and beat her for an unmerciful wretch, until his infant falls a lifeless lump at her feet! Can the Americans escape God Almighty? If they do, can he be to us a God of Justice? God is just, and I know it—for he has convinced me to my satisfaction—I cannot doubt him. My observer may see fathers beating their sons, mothers their daughters, and children their parents, all to pacify the passions of unrelenting tyrants. He may also, see them telling news and lies, making mischief one upon another. These are some of the productions of ignorance, which he will see practised among my dear brethren, who are held in unjust slavery and wretchedness, by avaricious and unmerciful tyrants, to whom, and their hellish deeds, I would suffer my life to be taken before I would submit. And when my curious observer comes to take notice of those who are said to be free, (which assertion I deny) and who are making some frivolous pretentions to common sense, he will see that branch of ignorance among the slaves assuming a more cunning and deceitful course of procedure.—He may see some of my brethren in league with tyrants, selling their own brethren into *hell upon earth,* not dissimilar to the exhibitions in Africa, but in a more secret, servile and abject manner. Oh Heaven! I am full!!! I can hardly move my pen!!!! and as I expect some will try to put me to death, to strike terror into others, and to obliterate from their minds the notion of freedom, so as to keep my brethren the more secure in wretchedness, where they will be permitted to stay but a short time (whether tyrants believe it or not)—I shall give the world a development of facts, which are already witnessed in the courts of heaven. My observer may see some of those ignorant and treacherous creatures (coloured people) sneaking about in the large cities, endeavouring to find out all strange coloured people, where they work and where they reside, asking them questions, and trying to ascertain whether they are runaways or not, telling them, at the same time, that they always have been, are, and always will be, friends to their brethren; and, perhaps, that they themselves are absconders, and a thousand such treacherous lies to get the better information of

the more ignorant!!! There have been and are at this day
in Boston, New-York, Philadelphia, and Baltimore, coloured
men, who are in league with tyrants, and who receive a great
portion of their daily bread, of the moneys which they acquire from the blood and tears of their more miserable
brethren, whom they scandalously delivered into the hands
of our *natural enemies!!!!!!*[45]

To show the force of degraded ignorance and deceit
among us some farther, I will give here an extract from a
paragraph, which may be found in the Columbian Centinel[46] of this city, for September 9, 1829, on the first page of
which, the curious may find an article, headed

"AFFRAY AND MURDER."
"Portsmouth, (Ohio) Aug. 22, 1829.

"A most shocking outrage was committed in Kentucky,
about eight miles from this place, on 14th inst. A negro
driver, by the name of Gordon, who had purchased in Maryland about sixty negroes, was taking them, assisted by an
associate named Allen, and the wagoner who conveyed the
baggage, to the Mississippi. The men were hand-cuffed and
chained together, in the usual manner for driving those
poor wretches, while the women and children were suffered
to proceed without incumbrance. It appears that, by means
of a file the negroes, unobserved, had succeeded in separating the iron which bound their hands, in such a way as to be
able to throw them off at any moment. About 8 o'clock in the
morning, while proceeding on the state road leading from
Greenup to Vanceburg, two of them dropped their shackles
and commenced a fight, when the wagoner (Petit) rushed in
with his whip to compel them to desist. At this moment,
every negro was found to be perfectly at liberty; and one of
them seizing a club, gave Petit a violent blow on the head,
and laid him dead at his feet; and Allen, who came to his
assistance, met a similar fate, from the contents of a pistol
fired by another of the gang. Gordon was then attacked,
seized and held by one of the negroes, whilst another fired
twice at him with a pistol, the ball of which each time grazed
his head, but not proving effectual, he was beaten with clubs,

and left for dead. They then commenced pillaging the wagon, and with an axe split open the trunk of Gordon, and rifled it of the money, about $2,400. Sixteen of the negroes then took to the woods; Gordon, in the mean time, not being materially injured, was enabled, by the assistance of one of the women, to mount his horse and flee; pursued, however, by one of the gang on another horse, with a drawn pistol; fortunately he escaped with his life barely, arriving at a plantation, as the negro came in sight; who then turned about and retreated.

"The neighbourhood was immediately rallied, and a hot pursuit given—which, we understand, has resulted in the capture of the whole gang and the recovery of the greatest part of the money. Seven of the negro men and one woman, it is said were engaged in the murders, and will be brought to trial at the next court in Greenupsburg."

Here my brethren, I want you to notice particularly in the above article, the *ignorant* and *deceitful actions* of this coloured woman. I beg you to view it candidly, as for ETERNITY!!!! Here a *notorious wretch*, with two other confederates had SIXTY of them in a gang, driving them like *brutes*—the men all in chains and hand-cuffs, and by the help of God they got their chains and hand-cuffs thrown off, and caught two of the wretches and put them to death, and beat the other until they thought he was dead, and left him for dead; however, he deceived them, and rising from the ground, this *servile woman* helped him upon his horse, and he made his escape. Brethren, what do you think of this? Was it the natural *fine feelings* of this woman, to save such a wretch alive? I know that the blacks, take them half enlightened and ignorant, are more humane and merciful than the most enlightened and refined European that can be found in all the earth. Let no one say that I assert this because I am prejudiced on the side of my colour, and against the whites or Europeans. For what I write, I do it candidly, for my God and the good of both parties: Natural observations have taught me these things; there is a solemn awe in the hearts of the blacks, as it respects *murdering* men:* whereas the

---

*Which is the reason the whites take the advantage of us.

whites, (though they are great cowards) where they have the
advantage, or think that there are any prospects of getting
it, they murder all before them, in order to subject men to
wretchedness and degradation under them. This is the natural result of pride and avarice. But I declare, the actions of
this black woman are really insupportable. For my own part,
I cannot think it was any thing but servile deceit, combined
with the most gross ignorance: for we must remember that
humanity, kindness and the *fear of the Lord,* does not consist in
protecting *devils.* Here is a set of wretches, who had SIXTY of
them in a gang, driving them around the country like *brutes,*
to dig up gold and silver for them, (which they will get
enough of yet.) Should the lives of such creatures be spared?
Are God and Mammon in league? What has the Lord to do
with a gang of desperate wretches, who go *sneaking about the
country like robbers*—light upon his people wherever they can
get a chance, binding them with chains and hand-cuffs, beat
and murder them as they would *rattle-snakes?* Are they not
the Lord's enemies? Ought they not to be destroyed? Any
person who will save such wretches from destruction, is
fighting against the Lord, and will receive his just recompense. The black men acted like *blockheads.* Why did they not
make sure of the wretch? He would have made sure of them,
if he could. It is just the way with black men—eight white
men can frighten fifty of them; whereas, if you can only get
courage into the blacks, I do declare it, that one good black
man can put to death six white men; and I give it as a fact,
let twelve black men get well armed for battle, and they will
kill and put to flight fifty whites.—The reason is, the blacks,
once you get them started, they glory in death. The whites
have had us under them for more than three centuries, murdering, and treating us like brutes; and, as Mr. Jefferson
wisely said, they have never *found us out*—they do not know,
indeed, that there is an unconquerable disposition in the
breasts of the blacks, which, when it is fully awakened and
put in motion, will be subdued, only with the destruction of
the animal existence. Get the blacks started, and if you do
not have a gang of tigers and lions to deal with, I am a de-
ceiver of the blacks and of the whites. How sixty of them
could let that wretch escape unkilled, I cannot conceive—

they will have to suffer as much for the two whom, they secured, as if they had put one hundred to death: if you
commence, make sure work—do not trifle, for they will not
trifle with you—they want us for their slaves, and think nothing of murdering us in order to subject us to that wretched
condition—therefore, if there is an *attempt* made by us, kill
or be killed. Now, I ask you, had you not rather be killed
than to be a slave to a tyrant, who takes the life of your
mother, wife, and dear little children? Look upon your
mother, wife and children, and answer God Almighty; and
believe this, that it is no more harm for you to kill a man,
who is trying to kill you, than it is for you to take a drink of
water when thirsty; in fact, the man who will stand still and
let another murder him, is worse than an infidel, and, if he
has common sense, ought not to be pitied. The actions of
this deceitful and ignorant coloured woman, in saving the
life of a desperate wretch, whose avaricious and cruel object
was to drive her, and her companions in miseries, through
the country like cattle, to make his fortune on their car-
casses, are but too much like that of thousands of our brethren in these states: if any thing is whispered by one, which
has any allusion to the melioration of their dreadful condition, they run and tell tyrants, that they may be enabled to
keep them the longer in wretchedness and miseries. Oh! coloured people of these United States, I ask you, in the name
of that God who made us, have we, in consequence of oppression, nearly lost the spirit of man, and, in no very
trifling degree, adopted that of brutes? Do you answer,
no?—I ask you, then, what set of men can you point me to,
in all the world, who are so abjectly employed by their oppressors, as we are by our *natural enemies?* How can, Oh! how
can those enemies but say that we and our children are not
of the HUMAN FAMILY, but were made by our Creator to be
an inheritance to them and theirs for ever? How can the
slaveholders but say that they can bribe the best coloured
person in the country, to sell his brethren for a trifling sum
of money, and take that atrocity to confirm them in their
avaricious opinion, that we were made to be slaves to them
and their children? How could Mr. Jefferson but say,*[47] "I

*See his Notes on Virginia, page 213.

advance it therefore as a suspicion only, that the blacks, whether originally a distinct race, or made distinct by time and circumstances, are *inferior* to the whites in the endowments both of body and mind?"—"It," says he, "is not against experience to suppose, that different species of the same genius, or varieties of the same species, may possess different qualifications." [Here, my brethren, listen to him.] ☞"Will not a lover of natural history, then, one who views the gradations in all the races of *animals* with the eye of philosophy, excuse an effort to keep those in the department of MAN as *distinct* as nature has formed them?"—I hope you will try to find out the meaning of this verse—its widest sense and all its bearings: whether you do or not, remember the whites do. This very verse, brethren, having emanated from Mr. Jefferson, a much greater philosopher the world never afforded, has in truth injured us more, and has been as great a barrier to our emancipation as any thing that has ever been advanced against us. I hope you will not let it pass unnoticed. He goes on further, and says: "This *unfortunate* difference of colour, and *perhaps* of *faculty,* is a powerful obstacle to the emancipation of these people. Many of their advocates, while they wish to vindicate the liberty of human nature are anxious also to preserve its *dignity* and *beauty.* Some of these, embarrassed by the question, 'What further is to be done with them?' join themselves in opposition with those who are actuated by sordid avarice only." Now I ask you candidly, my suffering brethren in time, who are candidates for the eternal worlds, how could Mr. Jefferson but have given the world these remarks respecting us, when we are so submissive to them, and so much servile deceit prevail among ourselves—when we so *meanly* submit to their murderous lashes, to which neither the Indians nor any other people under Heaven would submit? No, they would die to a man, before they would suffer such things from men who are no better than themselves, and *perhaps not so good.* Yes, how can our friends but be embarrassed, as Mr. Jefferson says, by the question, "What further is to be done with these people?" For while they are working for our emancipation, we are, by our treachery, wickedness and deceit, working against ourselves and our children—helping ours, and the enemies of God, to keep us and our dear little children in their infernal chains of slavery!!! Indeed, our friends cannot but relapse and join themselves "with those who are actuated by *sordid avarice* only!!!!" For my own part, I am glad Mr. Jefferson has advanced his positions for your sake; for you will either have to contradict or confirm him by your own actions, and not by what our friends have said or done for us; for those things are other men's labours, and do not satisfy the Americans, who are waiting for us to prove to them ourselves, that we are MEN, before they will be willing to admit the fact; for I pledge you my sacred word of honour, that Mr. Jefferson's remarks respecting us, have sunk deep into the hearts of millions of the whites, and never will be removed this side of eternity.—For how can they, when we are confirming him every day, by our *groveling submissions* and *treachery?* I aver, that when I look over these United States of America, and the world, and see the ignorant deceptions and consequent wretchedness of my brethren, I am brought oftimes solemnly to a stand, and in the midst of my reflections I exclaim to my God, "Lord didst thou make us to be slaves to our brethren, the whites?" But when I reflect that God is just, and that millions of my wretched brethren would meet death with glory—yea, more, would plunge into the very mouths of cannons and be torn into particles as minute as the atoms which compose the elements of the earth, in preference to a mean submission to the lash of tyrants, I am with streaming eyes, compelled to shrink back into nothingness before my Maker, and exclaim again, thy will be done, O Lord God Almighty.

Men of colour, who are also of sense, for you particularly is my APPEAL designed. Our more ignorant brethren are not able to penetrate its value. I call upon you therefore to cast your eyes upon the wretchedness of your brethren, and to do your utmost to enlighten them—*go to work and enlighten your brethren!*—Let the Lord see you doing what you can to rescue them and yourselves from degradation. Do any of you say that you and your family are free and happy, and what have you to do with the wretched slaves and other people? So can I say, for I enjoy as much freedom as any of you, if I am not quite as well off as the best of you. Look into our freedom and happiness, and see of what kind they are composed!! They are of the very lowest kind—they are the very *dregs!*—they are the most servile and abject kind, that ever a people was in possession of! If any of you wish to know how FREE you are, let one of you start and go through the southern and western States of this country, and unless you travel as a slave to a white man (a servant is a *slave* to the man whom he serves) or have your free papers, (which if you are not careful they will get from you) if they do not take you up and put you in jail, and if you cannot give good evidence of your freedom, sell you into eternal slavery, I am not a living man: or any man of colour, immaterial who he is, or where he came from, if he is not *the fourth from the negro race!!* (as we are called) the white Christians of America will serve him the same they will sink him into wretchedness and degradation for ever while he lives. And yet some of you have the hardihood to say that you are free and happy! May God have mercy on your freedom and happiness!! I met a coloured man in the street a short time since, with a string of boots on his shoulders; we fell into conversation, and in course of which, I said to him, what a miserable set of people we are! He asked, why?—Said I, we are so subjected under the whites, that we cannot obtain the comforts of life, but by cleaning their boots and shoes, old clothes, waiting on them, shaving them &c. Said he, (with the boots on his shoulders) "I am completely happy!!! I never want to live any better or happier than when I can get a plenty of boots and shoes to clean!!!" Oh! how can those who are actuated by avarice only, but think, that our Creator made us to be an inheritance to them for ever, when they see that our greatest glory is centered in such mean and low objects? Understand me, brethren, I do not mean to speak against the occupations by which we acquire enough and sometimes scarcely that, to render ourselves and families comfortable through life. I am subjected to the same inconvenience, as you all.—My objections are, to our *glorying* and being *happy* in such low employments; for if we are men, we ought to be thankful to the Lord for the past, and for the future. Be looking forward with thankful hearts to higher attainments than *wielding the razor* and *cleaning boots and shoes.* The man whose aspirations are not *above,* and even *below* these, is indeed, ignorant and wretched enough. I advanced it therefore to you, not as a *problematical,* but as an unshaken and for ever immovable *fact,* that your full glory and happiness, as well as all other coloured people under Heaven, shall never be fully consummated, but with the *entire emancipation of your enslaved brethren all over the world.* You may therefore, go to work and do what you can to rescue, or join in with tyrants to oppress them and yourselves, until the Lord shall come upon you all like a thief in the night. For I believe it is the will of the Lord that our greatest happiness shall consist in working for the salvation of our whole body. When this is accomplished a burst of glory will shine upon you, which will indeed astonish you and the world. Do any of you say this never will be done? I assure you that God will accomplish it—if nothing else will answer, he will hurl tyrants and devils into *atoms* and make way for his people. But O my brethren! I say unto you again, you must go to work and prepare the way of the Lord.

There is a great work for you to do, as trifling as some of you may think of it. You have to prove to the Americans and the world, that we are MEN, and not *brutes,* as we have been represented, and by millions treated. Remember, to let the aim of your labours among your brethren, and particularly the youths, be the dissemination of education and religion.* It is lamentable, that many of our children go to school, from four until they are eight or ten, and sometimes fifteen years of age, and leave school knowing but a little more about the grammar of their language than a horse does about handling a musket—and not a few of them are really so ignorant, that they are unable to answer a person correctly, general questions in geography, and to hear them

---

*Never mind what the ignorant ones among us may say, many of whom when you speak to them for their good, and try to enlighten their minds, laugh at you, and perhaps tell you plump to your face, that they want no instruction from you or any other Niger, and all such aggravating language. Now if you are a man of understanding and sound sense, I conjure you in the name of the Lord, and of all that is good, to impute their actions to ignorance, and wink at their follies, and do your very best to get around them some way or other, for remember they are your brethren; and I declare to you that it is for your interests to teach and enlighten them.

read, would only be to disgust a man who has a taste for reading; which, to do well, as trifling as it may appear to some, (to the ignorant in particular) is a great part of learning. Some few of them, may make out to scribble tolerably well, over a half sheet of paper, which I believe has hitherto been a powerful obstacle in our way, to keep us from acquiring knowledge. An ignorant father, who knows no more than what nature has taught him, together with what little he acquires by the senses of hearing and seeing, finding his son able to write a neat hand, sets it down for granted that he has as good learning as any body; the young, ignorant gump, hearing his father or mother, who perhaps may be ten times more ignorant, in point of literature, than himself, extolling his learning, struts about, in the full assurance, that his attainments in literature are sufficient to take him through the world, when, in fact, he has scarcely any learning at all!!!!

I promiscuously fell in conversation once, with an elderly coloured man on the topics of education, and of the great prevalency of ignorance among us: Said he, "I know that our people are very ignorant but my son has a good education: I spent a great deal of money on his education: he can write as well as any white man, and I assure you that no one can fool him," &c. Said I, what else can your son do, besides writing a good hand? Can he post a set of books in a mercantile manner? Can he write a neat piece of composition in prose or in verse? To these interrogations he answered in the negative. Said I, did your son learn, while he was at school, the width and depth of English Grammar? To which he also replied in the negative, telling me his son did not learn those things. Your son, said I, then, has hardly any learning at all—he is almost as ignorant, and more so, than many of those who never went to school one day in all their lives. My friend got a little put out, and so walking off, said that his son could write as well as any white man. Most of the coloured people, when they speak of the education of one among us who can write a neat hand, and who perhaps knows nothing but to scribble and puff pretty fair on a small scrap of paper, immaterial whether his words are grammatical, or spelt correctly, or not; if it only looks beautiful, they say he has as good an education as any white man—he can write as well as any white man, &c. The poor, ignorant creature, hearing, this, he is ashamed, forever after, to let any person see him humbling himself to another for knowledge but going about trying to deceive those who are more ignorant than himself, he at last falls an ignorant victim to death in wretchedness. I pray that the Lord may undeceive my ignorant brethren, and permit them to throw away pretensions, and seek after the substance of learning. I would crawl on my hands and knees through mud and mire, to the feet of a learned man, where I would sit and humbly supplicate him to instil into me, that which neither devils nor tyrants could remove, only with my life—for coloured people to acquire learning in this country, makes tyrants quake and tremble on their sandy foundation. Why, what is the matter? Why, they know that their infernal deeds of cruelty will be made known to the world. Do you suppose one man of good sense and learning would submit himself, his father, mother, wife and children, to be slaves to a wretched man like himself, who, instead of compensating him for his labours, chains, hand-cuffs and beats him and family almost to death, leaving life enough in them, however, to work for, and call him master? No! no! he would cut his devilish throat from ear to ear, and well do slave-holders know it. The bare name of educating the coloured people, scares our cruel oppressors almost to death. But if they do not have enough to be frightened for yet, it will be, because they can always keep us ignorant, and because God approbates their cruelties, with which they have been for centuries murdering us. The whites shall have enough of the blacks, yet, as true as God sits on his throne in Heaven.

Some of our brethren are so very full of learning, that you cannot mention any thing to them which they do not know better than yourself!!—nothing is strange to them!!—they knew every thing years ago!—if any thing should be mentioned in company where they are, immaterial how important it is respecting us or the world, if they had not divulged it; they make light of it, and affect to have known it long before it was mentioned and try to make all in the room, or wherever you may be, believe that your conversation is

nothing!!—not worth hearing! All this is the result of ignorance and ill-breeding; for a man of good-breeding, sense
and penetration, if he had heard a subject told twenty times
over, and should happen to be in company where one
should commence telling it again, he would wait with pa-
tience on its narrator, and see if he would tell it as it was told
in his presence before—paying the most strict attention to
what is said, to see if any more light will be thrown on the
subject: for all men are not gifted alike in telling, or even
hearing the most simple narration. These ignorant, vicious,
and wretched men, contribute almost as much injury to our
body as tyrants themselves, by doing so much for the promotion of ignorance amongst us; for they, making such pretensions to knowledge, such of our youth as are seeking after
knowledge, and can get access to them, take them as criteri-
ons to go by, who will lead them into a channel, where, unless the Lord blesses them with the privilege of seeing their
folly, they will be irretrievably lost forever, while in time!!!

I must close this article by relating the very heart-rending
fact, that I have examined school-boys and young men of
colour in different parts of the country, in the most simple
parts of Murray's English Grammar,[48] and not more than
one in thirty was able to give a correct answer to my interrogations. If any one contradicts me, let him step out of his
door into the streets of Boston, New-York, Philadelphia, or
Baltimore, (no use to mention any other, for the Christians
are too charitable further south or west!)—I say, let him who
disputes me, step out of his door into the streets of either
of those four cities, and promiscuously collect one hundred
school-boys, or young men of colour, *who have been to school,*
and who are considered by the coloured people to have received an excellent education, because, perhaps, some of
them can write a good hand, but who, notwithstanding their
neat writing, may be almost as ignorant, in comparison, as a
horse.—And, I say it, he will hardly find (in this enlightened
day, and in the midst of this *charitable* people) five in one
hundred, who, are able to correct the false grammar of their
language.—The cause of this almost universal ignorance
among us, I appeal to our schoolmasters to declare. Here is
a fact, which I this very minute take from the mouth of a

young coloured man, who has been to school in this state (Massachusetts) nearly nine years, and who knows grammar this day, *nearly* as well as he did the day he first entered the schoolhouse, under a white master. This young man says: "My master would never allow me to study grammar." I asked him, why? "The school committee," said he "forbid the coloured children learning grammar—they would not allow any but the white children to study grammar." It is a notorious fact, that the major part of the white Americans, have, ever since we have been among them, tried to keep us ignorant, and make us believe that God made us and our children to be slaves to them and theirs.[49] *Oh! my God, have mercy on Christian Americans!!!*

ARTICLE III.

OUR WRETCHEDNESS IN CONSEQUENCE OF THE PREACHERS OF THE RELIGION OF JESUS CHRIST.

Religion, my brethren, is a substance of deep consideration among all nations of the earth. The Pagans have a kind, as well as the Mahometans, the Jews and the Christians. But pure and undefiled religion, such as was preached by Jesus Christ and his apostles, is hard to be found in all the earth. God, through his instrument, Moses, handed a dispensation of his Divine will, to the children of Israel after they had left Egypt for the land of Canaan or of Promise, who through hypocrisy, oppression and unbelief, departed from the faith.[50]—He then, by his apostles, handed a dispensation of his, together with the will of Jesus Christ, to the Europeans in Europe, who, in open violation of which, have made *merchandise* of us, and it does appear as though they take this very dispensation to aid them in their *infernal* depredations upon us. Indeed, the way in which religion was and is conducted by the Europeans and their descendants, one might believe it was a plan fabricated by themselves and the *devils* to oppress us. But hark! My master has taught me better than to believe it—he has taught me that his gospel as it was preached by himself and his apostles remains the same, notwithstanding Europe has tried to mingle blood and oppression with it.

It is well known to the Christian world, that Bartholomew Las Casas, that very very notoriously avaricious Catholic priest or preacher, and adventurer with Columbus in his second voyage, proposed to his countrymen, the Spaniards in Hispaniola to import the Africans from the Portuguese settlement in Africa, to dig up gold and silver, and work their plantations for them, to effect which, he made a voyage thence to Spain, and opened the subject to his master, Ferdinand then in declining health, who listened to the plan: but who died soon after, and left it in the hand of his successor, Charles V.*[51] This wretch, ("Las Casas, the Preacher,") succeeded so well in his plans of oppression, that in 1503, the first blacks had been imported into the new world. Elated with this success, and stimulated by sordid avarice only, he importuned Charles V. in 1511, to 'grant permission to a Flemish merchant, to import 4000 blacks at one time.† Thus we see, through the instrumentality of a pretended preacher of the gospel of Jesus Christ our common master, our wretchedness first commenced in America—where it has been continued from 1503, to this day, 1829. A period of three hundred and twenty-six years. But two hundred and nine, from 1620—when twenty of our fathers were brought into Jamestown, Virginia, by a Dutch man of war, and sold off like brutes to the highest bidders;[53] and there is not a doubt in my mind, but that tyrants are in hope to perpetuate our miseries under them and their children until the final

---

*See Butler's History of the United States, vol. 1, page 24.—See also, page 25.[52]

†It is not unworthy of remark, that the Portuguese and Spaniards, were among, if not the very first Nations upon Earth, about three hundred and fifty or sixty years ago—But see what those *Christians* have come to now in consequence of afflicting our fathers and us, who have never molested, or disturbed them or any other of the white *Christians*, but have they received one quarter of what the Lord will yet bring upon them, for the murders they have inflicted upon us?—They have had, and in some degree have now, sweet times on our blood and groans, the time however, of bitterness have sometime since commenced with them.—There is a God the Maker and preserver of all things, who will as sure as the world exists, give all his creatures their just recompense of reward in this and in the world to come,—we may fool or deceive, and keep each other in the most profound ignorance, beat murder and keep each other out of what is our lawful rights, or the rights of man, yet it is impossible for us to deceive or escape the Lord Almighty.

consumation of all things.—But if they do not get dreadfully deceived, it will be because God has forgotten them.

The Pagans, Jews and Mahometans try to make proselytes to their religions, and whatever human beings adopt their religions they extend to them their protection. But Christian Americans, not only hinder their fellow creatures, the Africans, but thousands of them *will absolutely beat a coloured person nearly to death, if they catch him on his knees, supplicating the throne of grace.*[54] This barbarous cruelty was by all the heathen nations of antiquity, and is by the Pagans, Jews and Mahometans of the present day, left entirely to Christian Americans to inflict on the Africans and their descendants, that their cup which is nearly full may be completed. I have known tyrants or usurpers of human liberty in different parts of this country to take their fellow creatures, the coloured people, and beat them until they would scarcely leave life in them; what for? Why they say "The black devils had the audacity to be found *making prayers and supplications to the God who made them!!!!*" Yes, I have known small collections of coloured people to have convened together, for no other purpose than to worship God Almighty, in spirit and in truth, to the best of their knowledge; when tyrants, calling themselves *patrols*, would also convene and wait almost in breathless silence for the poor coloured people to commence singing and praying to the Lord our God, as soon as they had commenced, the wretches would burst in upon them and drag them out and commence beating them as they would rattle-snakes—many of whom, they would beat so unmercifully, that they would hardly be able to crawl for weeks and sometimes for months. Yet the American ministers send out missionaries to convert the heathen, while they keep us and our children sunk at their feet in the most abject ignorance and wretchedness that ever a people was afflicted with since the world began. Will the Lord suffer this people to proceed much longer? Will he not stop them in their career? Does he regard the heathens abroad, more than the heathens among the Americans? Surely the Americans must believe that God is partial, notwithstanding his Apostle Peter, declared before Cornelius and others that he has no respect to persons, but in every nation he that feareth God and worketh righteousness is accepted with him.[55]—"The word," said he, "which God sent unto the children of Israel, preaching peace, by Jesus Christ, (he is Lord of all."*) Have not the Americans the Bible in their hands? Do they believe it? Surely they do not. See how they treat us in open violation of the Bible!! They no doubt will be greatly offended with me, but if God does not awaken them, it will be, because they are superior to other men, as they have represented themselves to be. Our divine Lord and Master said, "all things whatsoever ye would that men should do unto you, do ye even so unto them." But an American minister, with the Bible in his hand, holds us and our children in the most abject slavery and wretchedness. Now I ask them, would they like for us to hold them and their children in abject slavery and wretchedness? No, says one, that never can be done— you are too abject and ignorant to do it—you are not men— you were made to be slaves to us, to dig up gold and silver for us and our children. Know this, my dear sirs, that although you treat us and our children now, as you do your domestic beast—yet the final result of all future events are known but to God Almighty alone, who rules in the armies of heaven and among the inhabitants of the earth, and who dethrones one earthly king and sits up another, as it seemeth good in his holy sight. We may attribute these vicissitudes to what we please, but the God of armies and of justice rules in heaven and in earth, and the whole American people shall see and know it yet, to their satisfaction. I have known pretended preachers of the gospel of my Master, who not only held us as their natural inheritance, but treated us with as much rigor as any Infidel or Deist[56] in the world— just as though they were intent only on taking our blood and groans to glorify the Lord Jesus Christ. The wicked and ungodly, seeing their preachers treat us with so much cruelty, they say: our preachers, who must be right, if any body are, treat them like brutes, and why cannot we?—They think it is no harm to keep them in slavery and put the whip to them, and why cannot we do the same!—They being preachers of the gospel of Jesus Christ, if it were any harm, they

*See Acts of the Apostles, chap. x. v. 25–27.

would surely preach against their oppression and do their
utmost to erase it from the country; not only in one or two
cities, but one continual cry would be raised in all parts of
this confederacy, and would cease only with the complete
overthrow of the system of slavery, in every part of the country. But how far the American preachers are from preaching
against slavery and oppression, which have carried their
country to the brink of a precipice; to save them from plung-
ing down the side of which, will hardly be affected, will appear in the sequel of this paragraph, which I shall narrate
just as it transpired. I remember a Camp Meeting in South
Carolina, for which I embarked in a Steam Boat at Charleston, and having been five or six hours on the water, we at
last arrived at the place of hearing, where was a very great
concourse of people, who were no doubt, collected together
to hear the word of God, (that some had collected barely as
spectators to the scene, I will not here pretend to doubt,
however, that is left to themselves and their God.) Myself
and boat companions, having been there a little while, we
were all called up to hear; I among the rest went up and
took my seat—being seated, I fixed myself in a complete
position to hear the word of my Saviour and to receive such
as I thought was authenticated by the Holy Scriptures; but
to my no ordinary astonishment, our Reverend gentleman
got up and told us (coloured people) that slaves must be
obedient to their masters—must do their duty to their masters or be whipped—the whip was made for the backs of
fools, &c. Here I pause for a moment, to give the world time
to consider what was my surprise, to hear such preaching
from a minister of my Master, whose very gospel is that of
peace and not of blood and whips, as this pretended
preacher tried to make us believe. What the American
preachers can think of us, I aver this day before my God, I
have never been able to define. They have newspapers and
monthly periodicals, which they receive in continual succession, but on the pages of which, you will scarcely ever find a
paragraph respecting slavery, which is ten thousand times
more injurious to this country than all the other evils put
together; and which will be the final overthrow of its government, unless something is very speedily done; for their cup

is nearly full.—Perhaps they will laugh at or make light of this; but I tell you Americans! that unless you speedily alter your course, *you* and your *Country are gone!!!!!!* For God Almighty will tear up the very face of the earth!!! Will not that very remarkable passage of Scripture be fulfilled on Christian Americans? Hear it Americans!! "He that is unjust, let him be unjust still:—and he which is filthy, let him be filthy still: and he that is righteous, let him be righteous still: and he that is holy, let him be holy still."* I hope that the Americans may hear, but I am afraid that they have done us so much injury, and are so firm in the belief that our Creator made us to be an inheritance to them for ever, that their hearts will be hardened, so that their destruction may be sure. This language, perhaps is too harsh for the American's delicate ears. But Oh Americans! Americans!! I warn you in the name of the Lord, (whether you will hear, or forbear,) to repent and reform, or you are ruined!!! Do you think that our blood is hidden from the Lord, because you can hide it from the rest of the world, by sending out missionaries, and by your charitable deeds to the Greeks, Irish, &c.?[57] Will he not publish your secret crimes on the house top? Even here in Boston, pride and prejudice have got to such a pitch, that in the very houses erected to the Lord, they have built little places for the reception of coloured people, where they must sit during meeting, or keep away from the house of God, and the preachers say nothing about it[58]—much less go into the hedges and highways seeking the lost sheep of the house of Israel, and try to bring them in to their Lord and Master. There are not a more wretched, ignorant, miserable, and abject set of beings in all the world, than the blacks in the Southern and Western sections of this country, under tyrants and devils. The preachers of America cannot see them, but they can send out missionaries to convert the heathens, notwithstanding. Americans! unless you speedily alter your course of proceeding, if God Almighty does not stop you, I say it in his name, that you may go on and do as you please for ever, both in time and eternity—never fear any evil at all!!!!!!!!!

*See Revelation, chap. xxii. 11.

☞ ADDITION.—The preachers and people of the United States form societies against Free Masonry and Intemperance, and write against Sabbath breaking, Sabbath mails, Infidelity, &c. &c.[59] But the fountain head,* compared with which, all those other evils are comparatively nothing, and from the bloody and murderous head of which, they receive no trifling support, is hardly noticed by the Americans. This is a fair illustration of the state of society in this country—it shows what a bearing *avarice* has upon a people, when they are nearly given up by the Lord to a hard heart and a reprobate mind, in consequence of afflicting their fellow creatures. God suffers some to go on until they are ruined for ever!!!!! Will it be the case with the whites of the United States of America?—We hope not—we would not wish to see them destroyed notwithstanding, they have and do now treat us more cruel than any people have treated another, on this earth since it came from the hands of its Creator (with the exceptions of the French and the Dutch, they treat us nearly as bad as the Americans of the United States.) The will of God must however, in spite of us, *be done.*

The English are the best friends the coloured people have upon earth.[60] Though they have oppressed us a little and have colonies now in the West Indies, which oppress us *sorely.*—Yet notwithstanding they (the English) have done one hundred times more for the melioration of our condition, than all the other nations of the earth put together. The blacks cannot but respect the English as a nation, notwithstanding they have treated us a little cruel.

There is no intelligent *black man* who knows any thing, but esteems a real Englishman, let him see him in what part of the world he will—for they are the greatest benefactors we have upon earth. We have here and there, in other nations, good friends. But as a nation, the English are our friends. ☜

How can the preachers and people of America believe the Bible? Does it teach them any distinction on account of a man's colour? Hearken, Americans! to the injunctions of our Lord and Master, to his humble followers.

*Slavery and oppression.

*"And Jesus came and spake unto them, saying, all power is given unto me in Heaven and in earth.

"Go ye, therefore, and teach all nations, baptizing them in the name of the Father, and of the Son, and of the Holy Ghost.

"Teaching them to observe all things whatsoever I have commanded you; and lo, I am with you alway, even unto the end of the world. Amen."

I declare, that the very face of these injunctions appear to be of God and not of man. They do not show the slightest degree of distinction. "Go ye therefore," (says my divine Master) "and teach all nations," (or in other words, all people) "baptizing them in the name of the Father, and of the Son, and of the Holy Ghost." Do you understand the above, Americans? We are a people, notwithstanding many of you doubt it. You have the Bible in your hands, with this very injunction.—Have you been to Africa, teaching the inhabitants thereof the words of the Lord Jesus? "Baptizing them in the name of the Father, and of the Son and of the Holy Ghost." Have you not, on the contrary, entered among us, and learnt us the art of throat-cutting, by setting us to fight, one against another, to take each other as prisoners of war, and sell to you for small bits of calicoes, old swords, knives, &c. to make slaves for you and your children? This being done, have you not brought us among you, in chains and hand-cuffs, like brutes, and treated us with all the cruelties and rigour your ingenuity could invent, consistent with the laws of your country, which (for the blacks) are tyrannical enough? Can the American preachers appeal unto God, the Maker and Searcher of hearts, and tell him, with the Bible in their hands, that they make no distinction on account of men's colour? Can they say, O God! thou knowest all things—thou knowest that we make no distinction between thy creatures, to whom we have to preach thy Word? Let them answer the Lord; and if they cannot do it in the affirmative, have they not departed from the Lord Jesus Christ, their master? But some may say, that they never had,

*See St. Matthew's Gospel, chap. xxviii. 18, 19, 20. After Jesus was risen from the dead.

or were in possession of religion, which made no distinction, and of course they could not have departed from it. I ask you then, in the name of the Lord, of what kind can your religion be? Can it be that which was preached by our Lord Jesus Christ from Heaven? I believe you cannot be so wicked as to tell him that his Gospel was that of *distinction*. What can the American preachers and people take God to be? Do they believe his words? If they do, do they believe that he will be mocked? Or do they believe, because they are whites and we blacks, that God will have respect to them? Did not God make us all as it seemed best to himself? What right, then, has one of us, to despise another, and to treat him cruel, on account of his colour, which none, but the God who made it can alter? Can there be a greater absurdity in nature, and particularly in a free republican country? But the Americans, having introduced slavery among them, their hearts have become almost seared, as with an hot iron, and God has nearly given them up to believe a lie in preference to the truth!!! And I am awfully afraid that pride, prejudice, avarice and blood, will, before long prove the final ruin of this happy republic, or land of *liberty!!!!* Can any thing be a greater mockery of religion than the way in which it is conducted by the Americans? It appears as though they are bent only on daring God Almighty to do his best—they chain and handcuff us and our children and drive us around the country like brutes, and go into the house of the God of justice to return him thanks for having aided them in their infernal cruelties inflicted upon us. Will the Lord suffer this people to go on much longer, taking his holy name in vain? Will he not stop them, PREACHERS and all? O Americans! Americans!! I call God—I call angels—I call men, to witness, that your DESTRUCTION *is at hand,* and will be speedily consummated unless you REPENT.

ARTICLE IV.

OUR WRETCHEDNESS IN CONSEQUENCE OF THE COLONIZING PLAN.

My dearly beloved brethren:—This is a scheme on which so many able writers, together with that very judicious coloured Baltimorean,[61] have commented, that I feel my delicacy about touching it. But as I am compelled to do the will of my Master, I declare, I will give you my sentiments upon it.—Previous, however, to giving my sentiments, either for or against it, I shall give that of Mr. Henry Clay,[62] together with that of Mr. Elias B. Caldwell, Esq. of the District of Columbia,[63] as extracted from the National Intelligencer,[64] by Dr. Torrey, author of a series of "Essays on Morals, and the Diffusion of Useful Knowledge."[65]

At a meeting which was convened in the District of Columbia, for the express purpose of agitating the subject of colonizing us in some part of the world,[66] Mr. Clay was called to the chair, and having been seated a little while, he rose and spake, in substance, as follows: says he—*"That class of the mixt population of our country [coloured people] was peculiarly situated; they neither enjoyed the immunities of freemen, nor were they subjected to the incapacities of slaves, but partook, in some degree, of the qualities of both. From their condition, and the unconquerable prejudices re-

*See Dr. Torrey's Portraiture of Domestic Slavery in the United States, pages 85, 86.

sulting from their colour, they never could amalgamate with the free whites of this country. It was desirable, therefore, as it respected them, and the residue of the population of the country, to drain them off. Various schemes of colonization had been thought of, and a part of our continent, it was supposed by some, might furnish a suitable establishment for them. But, for his part, Mr. C. said, he had a decided preference for some part of the Coast of Africa. There ample provision might be made for the colony itself, and it might be rendered instrumental to the introduction into that extensive quarter of the globe, of the arts, civilization, and Christianity." [Here I ask Mr. Clay, what kind of Christianity? Did he mean such as they have among the Americans— distinction, whip, blood and oppression? I pray the Lord Jesus Christ to forbid it.] "There," said he, "was a peculiar, a moral fitness, in restoring them to the land of their fathers, and if instead of the evils and sufferings which we had been the innocent cause of inflicting upon the inhabitants of Africa, we can transmit to her the blessings of our arts, our civilization, and our religion. May we not hope that America will extinguish a great portion of that moral debt which she has contracted to that unfortunate continent? Can there be a nobler cause than that which, whilst it proposes," &c. ******* [you know what this means.] "contemplates the spreading of the arts of civilized life, and the possible redemption from ignorance and barbarism of a benighted quarter of the globe?"

Before I proceed any further, I solicit your notice, brethren, to the foregoing part of Mr. Clay's speech, in which he says, (☞look above) "and if, instead of the evils and sufferings, which we had been the innocent cause of inflicting," &c.—What this very learned statesman could have been thinking about, when he said in his speech, "we had been the innocent cause of inflicting," &c., I have never been able to conceive. Are Mr. Clay and the rest of the Americans, innocent of the blood and groans of our fathers and us, their children?—Every individual may plead innocence, if he pleases, but God will, before long, separate the innocent from the guilty, unless something is speedily done—which I suppose will hardly be, so that their destruction may be sure.

bring up argument of opposing side

religion

Oh Americans! let me tell you, in the name of the Lord, it will be good for you, if you listen to the voice of the Holy Ghost, but if you do not, you are ruined!!! Some of you are good men; but the will of my God must be done. Those avaricious and ungodly tyrants among you, I am awfully afraid will drag down the vengeance of God upon you. When God Almighty commences his battle on the continent of America, for the oppression of his people, tyrants will wish they never were born.

But to return to Mr. Clay, whence I digressed. He says, "It was proper and necessary distinctly to state, that he understood it constituted no part of the object of this meeting, to touch or agitate in the slightest degree, a delicate question, connected with another portion of the coloured population of our country. It was not proposed to deliberate upon or consider at all, any question of emancipation, or that which was connected with the abolition of slavery. It was upon that condition alone, he was sure, that many gentlemen from the South and the West, whom he saw present, had attended, or could be expected to co-operate. It was upon that condition only, that he himself had attended."— That is to say, to fix a plan to get those of the coloured people, who are said to be free, away from among those of our brethren whom they unjustly hold in bondage, so that they may be enabled to keep them the more secure in ignorance and wretchedness, to support them and their children, and consequently they would have the more obedient slaves. For if the free are allowed to stay among the slaves, they will have intercourse together, and, of course, the free will learn the slaves _bad habits,_ by teaching them that they are MEN, as well as other people, and certainly _ought_ and _must_ be FREE.

I presume, that every intelligent man of colour must have some idea of Mr. Henry Clay, originally of Virginia, but now of Kentucky; they know too, perhaps, whether he is a friend, or a foe to the coloured citizens of this country, and of the world. This gentleman, according to his own words, had been highly favoured and blessed of the Lord, though he did not acknowledge it; but, to the contrary, he acknowledged men, for all the blessings with which God had favoured him. At a public dinner, given him at Fowler's

Garden,[67] Lexington, Kentucky, he delivered a public speech to a very large concourse of people—in the concluding clause of which, he says, "And now, my friends and fellow citizens, I cannot part from you, on possibly the last occasion of my ever publicly addessing you, without reiterating the expression of my thanks, from a heart overflowing with gratitude. I came among you, now more than thirty years ago, an orphan boy, pennyless, a stranger to you all, without friends, without the favour of the great, you took me up, cherished me, protected me, honoured me, you have constantly poured upon me a bold and unabated stream of innumerable favours, time which wears out every thing has increased and strengthened your affection for me. When I seemed deserted by almost the whole world, and assailed by almost every tongue, and pen, and press, you have fearlessly and manfully stood by me, with unsurpassed zeal and undiminished friendship. When I felt as if I should sink beneath the storm of abuse and detraction, which was violently raging around me, I have found myself upheld and sustained by your encouraging voices and approving smiles. I have doubtless, committed many faults and indiscretions, over which you have thrown the broad mantle of your charity. But I can say, and in the presence of God and in this assembled multitude, I will say, that I have honestly and faithfully served my country—that I have never wronged it—and that, however unprepared, I lament that I am to appear in the Divine presence on other accounts, I invoke the stern justice of his judgment on my public conduct, without the slightest apprehension of his displeasure."

Hearken to this Statesman indeed, but no philanthropist, whom God sent into Kentucky, an orphan boy, pennyless, and friendless, where he not only gave him a plenty of friends and the comforts of life, but raised him almost to the very highest honour in the nation, where his great talents, with which the Lord has been pleased to bless him, has gained for him the affection of a great portion of the people with whom he had to do. But what has this gentleman done for the Lord, after having done so much for him? The Lord has a suffering people, whose moans and groans at his feet for deliverance from oppression and wretchedness, pierce the very throne of Heaven, and call loudly on the God of Justice, to be revenged. Now, what this gentleman, who is so highly favoured of the Lord, has done to liberate those miserable victims of oppression, shall appear before the world, by his letters to Mr. Gallatin, Envoy Extraordinary and Minister Plenipotentiary to Great Britain, dated June 19, 1826.[68]—Though Mr. Clay was writing for the States, yet nevertheless, it appears, from the very face of his letters to that gentleman, that he was as anxious, if not more so, to get those free people and sink them into wretchedness, as his constituents, for whom he wrote.

The Americans of North and of South America, including the West India Islands—no trifling portion of whom were, for stealing, murdering, &c. compelled to flee from Europe, to save their necks or banishment, have effected their escape to this continent, where God blessed them with all the comforts of life—He gave them a plenty of every thing calculated to do them good—not satisfied with this, however, they wanted slaves, and wanted us for their slaves, who belong to the Holy Ghost, and no other, who we shall have to serve instead of tyrants.—I say, the Americans want us, the property of the Holy Ghost, to serve them. But there is a day fast approaching, when (unless there is a universal repentance on the part of the whites, which will scarcely take place, they have got to be so hardened in consequence of our blood, and so wise in their own conceit.) To be plain and candid with you, Americans! I say that the day is fast approaching, when there will be a greater time on the continent of America, than ever was witnessed upon this earth, since it came from the hand of its Creator. Some of you have done us so much injury, that you will never be able to repent.— Your cup must be filled.—You want us for your slaves, and shall have enough of us—God is just, *who will give you your fill of us.* But Mr. Henry Clay, speaking to Mr. Gallatin, respecting coloured people, who had effected their escape from the U. States (or to them *hell upon earth!!!*) to the hospitable shores of Canada,* from whence it would cause more than the lives of the Americans to get them, to plunge into

*Among the English, our real friends and benefactors.

wretchedness—he says: "The General Assembly of Kentucky, one of the states which is most affected by the escape of slaves into Upper Canada, has again, at their session which has just terminated, invoked the interposition of the General Government. In the treaty which has been recently concluded with the United Mexican States, and which is now under the consideration of the Senate, provision is made for the restoration of fugitive slaves. As it appears from your statements of what passed on that subject, with the British Plenipotentiaries, that they admitted the correctness of the principle of restoration, it is hoped that you will be able to succeed in making satisfactory arrangements."

There are a series of these letters, all of which are to the same amount; some however, presenting a face more of his own responsibility. I wonder what would this gentleman think, if the Lord should give him among the rest of his blessings enough of slaves? Could he blame any other being but himself? Do we not belong to the Holy Ghost? What business has he or any body else, to be sending letters about the world respecting us? Can we not go where we want to, as well as other people, only if we obey the voice of the Holy Ghost? This gentleman, (Mr. Henry Clay) not only took an active part in this colonizing plan, but was absolutely chairman of a meeting held at Washington, the 21st day of December 1816,* to agitate the subject of colonizing us in Africa.[69]—Now I appeal and ask every citizen of these United States and of the world, both *white* and *black,* who has any knowledge of Mr. Clay's public labor for these States—I want you candidly to answer the Lord, who sees the secrets of our hearts.—Do you believe that Mr. Henry Clay, late Secretary of State, and now in Kentucky, is a friend to the blacks, further, than his personal interest extends? Is it not his greatest object and glory upon earth, to sink us into miseries and wretchedness by making slaves of us, to work his plantation to enrich him and his family? Does he care a pinch of snuff about Africa—whether it remains a land of Pagans and of blood, or of Christians, so long as he gets

---

*In the first edition of this work, it should read 1816, as above, and not 1826, as it there appears.

enough of her sons and daughters to dig up gold and silver for him? If he had no slaves, and could obtain them in no other way if it were not, repugnant to the laws of his country, which prohibit the importation of slaves (which act was, indeed, more through apprehension than humanity) would he not try to import a few from Africa, to work his farm? Would he work in the hot sun to earn his bread, if he could make an African work for nothing, particularly, if he could keep him in ignorance and make him believe that God made him for nothing else but to work for him? Is not Mr. Clay a white man, and too delicate to work in the hot sun!! Was he not made by his Creator to sit in the shade, and make the blacks work without remuneration for their services, to support him and his family!!! I have been for some time taking notice of this man's speeches and public writings, but never to my knowledge have I seen any thing in his writings, which insisted on the emancipation of slavery, which has almost ruined his country. Thus we see the depravity of men's hearts, when in pursuit only of gain—particularly when they oppress their fellow creatures to obtain that gain—God suffers some to go on until they are lost forever. This same Mr. Clay, wants to know, what he has done, to merit the disapprobation of the American people. In a public speech delivered by him, he asked: "Did I involve my country in an unnecessary war?" to merit the censure of the Americans—"Did I bring obliquy upon the nation, or the people whom I represented?—did I ever lose any opportunity to advance the fame, honor and prosperity of this State and the Union?"[70] How astonishing it is, for a man who knows so much about God and his ways, as Mr. Clay, to ask such frivolous questions? Does he believe that a man of his talents and standing in the midst of a people, will get along unnoticed by the penetrating and all seeing eye of God, who is continually taking cognizance of the hearts of men? Is not God against him, for advocating the murderous cause of slavery? If God is against him, what can the Americans, together with the whole world do for him? Can they save him from the hand of the Lord Jesus Christ?

I shall now pass in review the speech of Mr. Elias B. Caldwell, Esq. of the District of Columbia, extracted from the same page on which Mr. Clay's will be found. Mr. Caldwell, giving his opinion respecting us, at that ever memorable meeting, he says: "The more you improve the condition of these people, the more you cultivate their minds, the more miserable you make them in their present state. You give them a higher relish for those privileges which they can never attain, and turn what we intend for a blessing into a curse." Let me ask this benevolent man, what he means by a blessing intended for us? Did he mean sinking us and our children into ignorance and wretchedness, to support him and his family? What he meant will appear evident and obvious to the most ignorant in the world ☞ See Mr. Caldwell's intended blessings for us, O! my Lord!! "No," said he, "if they must remain in their present situation, keep them in the *lowest state of degradation and ignorance.* The nearer you bring them to the condition of brutes, the better chance do you give them of possessing their *apathy.*" Here I pause to get breath, having labored to extract the above clause of this gentleman's speech, at that colonizing meeting. I presume that everybody knows the meaning of the word *"apathy,"*—if any do not, let him get Sheridan's Dictionary, in which he will find it explained in full.[71] I solicit the attention of the world, to the foregoing part of Mr. Caldwell's speech, that they may see what man will do with his fellow men, when he has them under his feet. To what length will not man go in iniquity when given up to a hard heart, and reprobate mind, in consequence of blood and oppression? The last clause of this speech, which was written in a very artful manner, and which will be taken for the speech of a friend, without close examination and deep penetration, I shall now present. He says, "surely, Americans ought to be the last people on earth, to advocate such slavish doctrines, to cry peace and contentment to those who are deprived of the privileges of civil liberty, they who have so largely partaken of its blessings, who know so well how to estimate its value, ought to be among the foremost to extend it to others." The real sense and meaning of the last part of Mr. Caldwell's speech is, get the free people of colour away to Africa, from among the slaves, where they may at once be blessed and happy, and those who we hold in slavery, will be contented to rest in ignorance and wretchedness, to dig up gold and silver for us and our children. Men have indeed got to be so cunning, these days, that it would take the eye of a Solomon[72] to penetrate and find them out.

☞ ADDITION.—Our dear Redeemer said, "Therefore, whatsoever ye have spoken in darkness, shall be heard in the light; and that which ye have spoken in the ear in closets, shall be proclaimed upon the house tops."[73]

How obviously this declaration of our Lord has been shown among the Americans of the United States. They have hitherto passed among some nations, who do not know any thing about their internal concerns, for the most enlightened, humane, charitable, and merciful people upon earth, when at the same time they treat us, the (coloured people) secretly more cruel and unmerciful than any other nation upon earth.—It is a fact, that in our Southern and Western States, there are millions who hold us in chains or in slavery, whose greatest object and glory, is centered in keeping us sunk in the most profound ignorance and stupidity, to make us work without remunerations for our services. Many of whom if they catch a coloured person, whom they hold in unjust ignorance, slavery and degradation, to them and their children, with a book in his hand, will beat him nearly to death. I heard a wretch in the state of North Carolina said, that if any man would teach a black person whom he held in slavery, to spell, read or write, he would prosecute him to the very extent of the law.—Said the ignorant wretch,* "a Nigar, ought not to have any more sense than enough to work for his master." May I not ask to fatten the wretch and his family?—These and similar cruelties these *Christians* have been for hundreds of years inflicting on our fathers and us in the dark, God has however, very recently published some of their secret crimes on the house top, that the world may gaze on their Christianity and see of what kind it is composed.—Georgia for instance, God has com-

---

*It is a fact, that in all our Slave-holding States (in the countries) there are thousands of the whites, who are almost as ignorant in comparison as horses, the most they know, is to beat the coloured people, which some of them shall have their hearts full of yet.

pletely shown to the world, the *Christianity* among its white *inhabitants*. A law has recently passed the Legislature of this *republican* State (Georgia) prohibiting all free or slave persons of colour, from learning to read or write; another law has passed the *republican* House of Delegates, (but not the Senate) in Virginia, to prohibit all persons of colour, (free and slave) from learning to read or write, and even to hinder them from meeting together in order to worship our Maker!!!!!![74]—Now I solemnly appeal, to the most skilful historians in the world, and all those who are mostly acquainted with the histories of the Antideluvians[75] and of Sodom and Gomorrah,[76] to show me a parallel of barbarity. *Christians!! Christians!!!* I dare you to show me a parallel of cruelties in the annals of Heathens or of Devils, with those of Ohio,[77] Virginia and of Georgia—know the world that these things were before done in the dark, or in a corner under a garb of humanity and religion. God has however, taken of the fig-leaf covering, and made them expose themselves on the house top. I tell you that God works in many ways his wonders to perform, he will unless they repent, make them expose themselves enough more yet to the world.—See the acts of the *Christians* in FLORIDA, SOUTH CAROLINA, and KENTUCKY[78]—was it not for the reputation of the house of my Lord and Master, I would mention here, an act of cruelty inflicted a few days since on a black man, by the white *Christians* in the PARK STREET CHURCH,[79] in this (CITY) which is almost enough to make Demons themselves quake and tremble in their FIREY HABITATIONS.—Oh! my Lord how refined in iniquity the whites have got to be in consequence of our blood*—what kind!! Oh! what kind!!! of Christianity can be found this day in all the earth!!!!!!

I write without the fear of man, I am writing for my God, and fear none but himself; they may put me to death if they choose—(I fear and esteem a good man however, let him be black or white.) I forbear to comment on the cruelties in-

---

*The Blood of our fathers who have been murdered by the whites, and the groans of our Brethren, who are now held in cruel ignorance, wretchedness and slavery by them, cry aloud to the Maker of Heaven and of earth, against the whole continent of America, for redresses.

flicted on this Black Man by the Whites, in the Park Street
MEETING HOUSE, I will leave it in the dark!!!!! But I declare
that the atrocity is really to Heaven daring and infernal, that
I must say that God has commenced a course of exposition
among the Americans, and the glorious and heavenly work
will continue to progress until they learn to do justice. ☜𝔒

Extract from the Speech of Mr. John Randolph, of Roanoke.[80]

Said he:—"It had been properly observed by the Chairman, as well as by the gentleman from this District (meaning
Messrs. Clay and Caldwell) that there was nothing in the
proposition submitted to consideration which in the smallest
degree touches another very important and delicate question, which ought to be left as much out of view as possible,
(Negro Slavery.)*

"There is no fear," Mr. R. said, "that this proposition
would alarm the slave-holders; they had been accustomed to
think seriously of the subject.—There was a popular work on
agriculture, by John Taylor of Carolina [Caroline], which was
widely circulated, and much confided in, in Virginia. In that
book, much read because coming from a practical man, this
description of people, [referring to us half free ones] were
pointed out as a great evil. They had indeed been held up
as the greater bug-bear to every man who feels an inclina-
tion to emancipate his slaves, not to create in the bosom of
his country so great a nuisance. If a place could be provided
for their reception, and a mode of sending them hence,
there were hundreds, nay thousands of citizens who would,
by manumitting their slaves, relieve themselves from the
cares attendant on their possession. The great slaveholder,"
Mr. R. said, "was frequently a mere sentry at his own door—
bound to stay on his plantation to see that his slaves were
properly treated, &c." Mr. R. concluded by saying, that he

---

*"Niger," is a word derived from the Latin, which was used by the old
Romans, to designate inanimate beings, which were black: such as soot,
pot, wood, house, &c. Also, animals which they considered inferior to the
human species, as a black horse, cow, hog, bird, dog, &c. The white Americans have applied this term to Africans, by way of reproach for our colour,
to aggravate and heighten our miseries, because they have their feet on our
throats.

had thought it necessary to make these remarks being a slaver-holder himself, to shew that, "so far from being connected with abolition of slavery, the measure proposed would prove one of the greatest securities to enable the master to keep in possession his own property."

Here is a demonstrative proof, of a plan got up, by a gang of slave-holders to select the free people of colour from among the slaves, that our more miserable brethren may be the better secured in ignorance and wretchedness, to work their farms and dig their mines, and thus go on enriching the Christians with their blood and groans. What our brethren could have been thinking about, who have left their native land and home and gone away to Africa, I am unable to say. This country is as much ours as it is the whites, whether they will admit it now or not, they will see and believe it by and by. They tell us about prejudice—what have we to do with it? Their prejudices will be obliged to fall like lightning to the ground, in succeeding generations; not, however, with the will and consent of all the whites, for some will be obliged to hold on to the old adage, viz: the blacks are not men, but were made to be an inheritance to us and our children for ever!!!!!! I hope the residue of the coloured people, will stand still and see the salvation of God and the miracle which he will work for our delivery from wretchedness under the Christians!!!!!!

☞ ADDITION.—If any of us see fit to go away, go to those who have been for many years, and are now our greatest earthly friends and benefactors—the English. If not so, go to our brethren, the Haytians, who, according to their word, are bound to protect and comfort us.[81] The Americans say, that we are ungrateful—but I ask them for heaven's sake, what should we be grateful to them for—for murdering our fathers and mothers?—Or do they wish us to return thanks to them for chaining and handcuffing us, branding us, cramming fire down our throats, or for keeping us in slavery, and beating us nearly or quite to death to make us work in ignorance and miseries, to support them and their families. They certainly think that we are a gang of fools. Those among them, who have volunteered their services for our redemption, though we are unable to compensate them for their labours, we nevertheless thank them from the bottom of our hearts, and have our eyes steadfastly fixed upon them, and their labours of love for God and man.—But do slave-holders think that we thank them for keeping us in miseries, and taking our lives by the inches? ༻

Before I proceed further with this scheme, I shall give an extract from the letter of that truly Reverend Divine, (Bishop Allen,) of Philadelphia,[82] respecting this trick. At the instance of the editor of the Freedom's Journal,[83] he says,* "Dear Sir, I have been for several years trying to reconcile my mind to the Colonizing of Africans in Liberia, but there have always been, and there still remain great and insurmountable objections against the scheme. We are an unlettered people, brought up in ignorance, not one in a hundred can read or write, not one in a thousand has a liberal education; is there any fitness for such to be sent into a far country, among heathens, to convert or civilize them, when they themselves are neither civilized or Christianized? See the great bulk of the poor, ignorant Africans in this country, exposed to every temptation before them: all for the want of their morals being refined by education and proper attendance paid unto them by their owners, or those who had the charge of them. It is said by the Southern slave-holders, that the more ignorant they can bring up the Africans, the better slaves they make, ("go and come.") Is there any fitness for such people to be colonized in a far country to be their own rulers? Can we not discern the project of sending the free people of colour away from their country? Is it not for the interest of the slave-holders to select the free people of colour out of the different states, and send them to Liberia? Will it not make their slaves uneasy to see free men of colour enjoying liberty? It is against the law in some of the Southern States, that a person of colour should receive an education, under a severe penalty. Colonizationists speak of America being first colonized; but is there any comparison between the two? America was colonized by as *wise, judicious* and *educated* men as the world afforded. WILLIAM PENN did not want for *learning, wisdom,* or *intelligence.* If all

*See Freedom's Journal for Nov. 2d, 1827—vol. 1, No. 34.

the people in Europe and America were as ignorant and in the same situation as our brethren, what would become of the world? Where would be the principle or piety that would govern the people? We were *stolen* from our mother country, and brought *here*. We have *tilled* the ground and made fortunes for thousands, and still they are not weary of our services. *But they who stay to till the ground must be slaves.* Is there not land enough in America, or "corn enough in Egypt?" Why should they send us into a far country to die? See the thousands of foreigners emigrating to America every year: and if there be ground sufficient for them to cultivate, and bread for them to eat, why would they wish to send the *first tillers* of the land away? Africans have made fortunes for thousands, who are yet unwilling to part with their services; but the free must be sent away, and those who remain, must be *slaves.* I have no doubt that there are many good men who do not see as I do, and who are for sending us to Liberia; but they have not duly considered the subject—they are not men of colour.—This land which we have watered with our *tears* and *our blood,* is now our *mother country,* and we are well satisfied to stay where wisdom abounds and the gospel is free.

> "RICHARD ALLEN,
> *"Bishop of the African Methodist Episcopal*
> *"Church in the United States."*

I have given you, my brethren, an extract verbatim, from the letter of that godly man, as you may find it on the aforementioned page of Freedom's Journal. I know that thousands, and perhaps millions of my brethren in these States, have never heard of such a man as Bishop Allen—a man whom God many years ago raised up among his ignorant and degraded brethren, to preach Jesus Christ and him crucified to them—who notwithstanding, had to wrestle against principalities and the powers of darkness to diffuse that gospel with which he was endowed among his brethren—but who having overcome the combined powers of devils and wicked men, has under God planted a Church among us which will be as durable as the foundation of the earth on which it stands.[84] Richard Allen! O my God!! The bare recollection of the labours of this man, and his ministers among his deplorably wretched brethren, (rendered so by the whites) to bring them to a knowledge of the God of Heaven, fills my soul with all those very high emotions which would take the pen of an Addison[85] to portray. It is impossible my brethren for me to say much in this work respecting that man of God. When the Lord shall raise up coloured historians in succeeding generations, to present the crimes of this nation, to the then gazing world, the Holy Ghost will make them do justice to the name of Bishop Allen, of Philadelphia. Suffice it for me to say, that the name of this very man (Richard Allen) though now in obscurity and degradation, will notwithstanding, stand on the pages of history among the greatest divines who have lived since the apostolic age, and among the Africans, Bishop Allen's will be entirely preeminent. My brethren, search after the character and exploits of this godly man among his ignorant and miserable brethren, to bring them to a knowledge of the truth as it is in our Master. Consider upon the tyrants and false Christians against whom he had to contend in order to get access to his brethren. See him and his ministers in the States of New York, New Jersey, Pennsylvania, Delaware and Maryland, carrying the gladsome tidings of free and full salvation to the coloured people. Tyrants and false Christians however, would not allow him to penetrate far into the South, for fear that he would awaken some of his ignorant brethren, whom they held in wretchedness and misery—for fear, I say it, that he would awaken and bring them to a knowledge of their Maker.[86] O my Master! my Master! I cannot but think upon Christian Americans!!!—What kind of people can they be? Will not those who were burnt up in Sodom and Gomorrah rise up in judgment against Christian Americans with the Bible in their hands, and condemn them? Will not the Scribes and Pharisees of Jerusalem,[87] who had nothing but the laws of Moses and the Prophets[88] to go by, rise up in judgment against Christian Americans, and condemn them,* who, in addition to these have a revelation

*I mean those whose labours for the good, or rather destruction of Jerusalem, and the Jews ceased before our Lord entered the Temple, and overturned the tables of the Money Changers.[89]

from Jesus Christ the Son of the living God? In fine, will not the Antideluvians, together with the whole heathen world of antiquity, rise up in judgment against Christian Americans and condemn them? The Christians of Europe and America go to Africa, bring us away, and throw us into the seas, and in other ways murder us, as they would wild beast. The Antideluvians and heathens never dreamed of such barbarities.— Now the Christians believe, because they have a name to live, while they are dead, that God will overlook such things. But if he does not deceive them, it will be because he has overlooked it sure enough. But to return to this godly man, Bishop Allen. I do hereby openly affirm it to the world, that he has done more in a spiritual sense for his ignorant and wretched brethren than any other man of colour has, since the world began. And as for the greater part of the whites, it has hitherto been their greatest object and glory to keep us ignorant of our Maker, so as to make us believe that we were made to be slaves to them and their children, to dig up gold and silver for them. It is notorious that not a few professing Christians among the whites, who profess to love our Lord and Saviour Jesus Christ, have assailed this man and laid all the obstacles in his way they possibly could, consistent with their profession—and what for? Why, their course of proceeding and his, clashed exactly together—they trying their best to keep us ignorant, that we might be the better and more obedient slaves—while he, on the other hand, doing his very best to enlighten us and teach us a knowledge of the Lord. And I am sorry that I have it to say, that many of our brethren have joined in with our oppressors, whose dearest objects are only to keep us ignorant and miserable against this man to stay his hand.—However, they have kept us in so much ignorance, that many of us know no better than to fight against ourselves, and by that means strengthen the hands of our natural enemies, to rivet their infernal chains of slavery upon us and our children. I have several times called the white Americans our *natural enemies*—I shall here define my meaning of the phrase. Shem, Ham and Japheth, together with their father Noah and wives, I believe were not natural enemies to each other.[90] When the ark rested after the flood upon Mount Arrarat, in Asia, they (eight) were all the people which could be found alive in all the earth[91]—in fact if Scriptures be true, (which I believe are) there were no other living men in all the earth, notwithstanding some ignorant creatures hesitate not to tell us that we, (the blacks) are the seed of Cain the murderer of his brother Abel.[92] But where or of whom those ignorant and avaricious wretches could have got their information, I am unable to declare. Did they receive it from the Bible? I have searched the Bible as well as they, if I am not as well learned as they are, and have never seen a verse which testifies whether we are the seed of Cain or of Abel. Yet those men tell us that we are the seed of Cain, and that God put a dark stain upon us, that we might be known as their slaves!!! Now, I ask those avaricious and ignorant wretches, who act more like the seed of Cain, by murdering the whites or the blacks? How many vessel loads of human beings, have the blacks thrown into the seas? How many thousand souls have the blacks murdered in cold blood, to make them work in wretchedness and ignorance, to support them and their families?*—However, let us be the seed of *Cain, Harry, Dick,* or *Tom!!!* God will show the whites what we are, yet. I say, from the beginning, I do not think that we were natural enemies to each other. But the whites having made us so wretched, by subjecting us to slavery, and having murdered so many millions of us, in order to make us work for them, and out of devilishness—and they taking our wives, whom we love as we do ourselves—our mothers, who bore the pains of death to give us birth—our fathers and dear little children, and ourselves, and strip and beat us one before the other—chain, hand-cuff, and drag us about like rattlesnakes—shoot us down like wild bears, before each other's faces, to make us submissive to, and work to support them and their families. They (the whites) know well, if we are *men*—and there is a secret monitor in their hearts which tells them we are—they know, I say, if we *are* men, and see them treating us in the manner they do, that

*How many millions souls of the human family have the blacks beat nearly to death, to keep them from learning to read the Word of God, and from writing. And telling lies about them, by holding them up to the world as a tribe of TALKING APES, void of INTELLECT!!!!! *incapable* of LEARNING, &c.

there can be nothing in our hearts but death alone, for them, notwithstanding we may appear cheerful, when we see them murdering our dear mothers and wives, because we cannot help ourselves. Man, in all ages and all nations of the earth, is the same. Man is a peculiar creature—he is the image of his God, though he may be subjected to the most wretched condition upon earth, yet the spirit and feeling which constitute the creature, man, can never be entirely erased from his breast, because the God who made him after his own image, planted it in his heart; he cannot get rid of it. The whites knowing this, they do not know what to do; they know that they have done us so much injury, they are afraid that we, being men, and not brutes, will retaliate, and woe will be to them; therefore, that dreadful fear, together with an avaricious spirit, and the natural love in them, to be called masters, (which term will yet honour them with to their sorrow) bring them to the resolve that they will keep us in ignorance and wretchedness, as long as they possibly can,* and make the best of their time, while it lasts. Consequently they, themselves, (and not us) render themselves our natural enemies, by treating us so cruel. They keep us miserable now, and call us their property, but some of them will have enough of us by and by—their stomachs shall run over with us; they want us for their slaves, and shall have us to their fill. We are all in the world together!!—I said above, because we cannot help ourselves, (viz. we cannot help the whites murdering our mothers and our wives) but this statement is incorrect—for we can help ourselves; for, if we lay

---

*And still holds us up with indignity as being incapable of acquiring knowledge!!! See the inconsistency of the assertions of those wretches—they beat us inhumanely, sometimes almost to death, for attempting to inform ourselves, by reading the *Word* of our Maker, and at the same time tell us, that we are beings *void of intellect!!!!* How admirably their practices agree with their professions in this case. Let me cry shame upon you Americans, for such outrages upon human nature!!! If it were possible for the whites always to keep us ignorant and miserable, and make us work to enrich them and their children, and insult our feelings by representing us as *talking Apes*, what would they do? But glory, honour and praise to Heaven's King, that the sons and daughters of Africa, will, in spite of all the opposition of their enemies, stand forth in all the dignity and glory that is granted by the Lord to his creature man.

aside abject servility, and be determined to act like men, and not brutes—the murderers among the whites would be afraid to show their cruel heads. But O, my God!—in sorrow I must say it, that my colour, all over the world, have a mean, servile spirit. They yield in a moment to the whites, let them be right or wrong—the reason they are able to keep their feet on our throats. Oh! my coloured brethren, all over the world, when shall we arise from this death-like apathy?— And be men!! You will notice, if ever we become men, (I mean *respectable* men, such as other people are,) we must exert ourselves to the full. For remember, that it is the greatest desire and object of the greater part of the whites, to keep us ignorant, and make us work to support them and their families.—Here now, in the Southern and Western sections of this country, there are at least three coloured persons for one white, why is it, that those few weak, good-for-nothing whites, are able to keep so many able men, one of whom, can put to flight a dozen whites, in wretchedness and misery? It shows at once, what the blacks are, we are ignorant, abject, servile and mean—and the whites know it—they know that we are too servile to assert our rights as men—or they would not fool with us as they do. Would they fool with any other peoples as they do with us? No, they know too well, that they would get themselves ruined. Why do they not bring the inhabitants of Asia to be body servants to them? They know they would get their bodies rent and torn from head to foot. Why do they not get the Aborigines of this country to be slaves to them and their children, to work their farms and dig their mines? They know well that the Aborigines of this country, or (Indians) would tear them from the earth. The Indians would not rest day or night, they would be up all times of night, cutting their cruel throats. But my colour, (some, not all,) are willing to stand still and be murdered by the cruel whites. In some of the West-Indies Islands, and over a large part of South America, there are six or eight coloured persons for one white.* Why

*For instance in the two States of Georgia, and South Carolina, there are, perhaps, not much short of six or seven hundred thousand persons of colour; and if I was a gambling character, I would not be afraid to stake down upon the board FIVE CENTS against TEN, that there are in the single

do they not take possession of those places? Who hinders them? It is not the avaricious whites—for they are too busily engaged in laying up money—derived from the blood and tears of the blacks. The fact is, they are too servile, they love to have Masters too well!! Some of our brethren, too, who seeking more after self aggrandisement, than the glory of God, and the welfare of their brethren, join in with our oppressors, to ridicule and say all manner of evils falsely against our Bishop. They think, that they are doing great things, when they can get in company with the whites, to ridicule and make sport of those who are labouring for their good. Poor ignorant creatures, they do not know that the sole aim and object of the whites, are only to make fools and slaves of them, and put the whip to them, and make them work to support them and their families. But I do say, that no man, can well be a despiser of Bishop Allen, for his public labours among us, unless he is a despiser of God and of

---

State of Virginia, five or six hundred thousand Coloured persons. Four hundred and fifty thousand of whom (let them be well equipt for war) I would put against every white person on the whole continent of America. (Why? why because I know that the Blacks, once they get involved in a war, had rather die than to live, they either kill or be killed.) The whites know this too, which make them quake and tremble. To show the world further, how servile the coloured people are, I will only hold up to view, the one Island of Jamaica, as a specimen of our meanness.

In that Island, there are three hundred and fifty thousand souls—of whom fifteen thousand are whites, the remainder, three hundred and thirty-five thousand are coloured people! and this Island is ruled by the white people!!!!!!!! (15,000) ruling and tyranizing over 335,000 persons!!!!!!!!—O! coloured men!! O! coloured men!!! O! coloured men!!!! Look!! look!!! at this!!!! and, tell me if we are not abject and servile enough, how long, O! how long my colour shall we be dupes and dogs to the cruel whites?—I only passed Jamaica, and its inhabitants, in review as a specimen to show the world, the condition of the Blacks at this time, now coloured people of the whole world, I beg you to look at the (15000 white,) and (Three Hundred and Thirty-five Thousand coloured people) in that Island, and tell me how can the white tyrants of the world but say that we are not men, but were made to be slaves and Dogs to them and their children forever!!!!!!!—why my friend only look at the thing!!!! (15000) whites keeping in wretchedness and degradation (335000) viz. 22 coloured persons for one white!!!!!!! when at the same time, an equal number (15000) Blacks, would almost take the whole of South America, because where they go as soldiers to fight death follows in their train.[93]

Righteousness. Thus, we see, my brethren, the two very opposite positions of those great men, who have written respecting this "Colonizing Plan." (Mr. Clay and his slave-
holding party,) men who are resolved to keep us in eternal
wretchedness, are also bent upon sending us to Liberia.
While the Reverend Bishop Allen, and his party, men who
have the fear of God, and the wellfare of their brethren at
heart. The Bishop, in particular, whose labours for the salvation of his brethren, are well known to a large part of those,
who dwell in the United States, are completely opposed to
the plan—and advise us to stay where we are. Now we have
to determine whose advice we will take respecting this all
important matter, whether we will adhere to Mr. Clay and
his slave holding party, who have always been our oppressors and murderers, and who are for colonizing us, more
through apprehension than humanity, or to this godly man
who has done so much for our benefit, together with the
advice of all the good and wise among us and the whites.
Will any of us leave our homes and go to Africa? I hope not.*
Let them commence their attack upon us as they did on our
brethren in Ohio, driving and beating us from our country,
and my soul for theirs, they will have enough of it. Let no
man of us budge one step, and let slave-holders come to beat
us from our country. America is more our country, than it is
the whites—we have enriched it with our *blood and tears.* The
greatest riches in all America have arisen from our blood
and tears:—and will they drive us from our property and
homes, which we have earned with our *blood?* They must
look sharp or this very thing will bring swift destruction
upon them. The Americans have got so fat on our blood and
groans, that they have almost forgotten the God of armies.
But let them go on.

---

*Those who are ignorant enough to go to Africa, the coloured people
ought to be glad to have them go, for if they are ignorant enough to let the
whites *fool* them off to Africa, they would be no small injury to us if they
reside in this country.

☞ ADDITION.—I will give here a very imperfect list of the cruelties inflicted on us by the enlightened Christians of America.—First, no trifling portion of them will beat us nearly to death, if they find us on our knees praying to God,—They hinder us from going to hear the word of God—they keep us sunk in ignorance, and will not let us learn to read the word of God, nor write—If they find us with a book of any description in our hand, they will beat us nearly to death—they are so afraid we will learn to read, and enlighten our dark and benighted minds—They will not suffer us to meet together to worship the God who made us—they brand us with hot iron—they cram bolts of fire down our throats—they cut us as they do horses, bulls, or hogs—they crop our ears and sometimes cut off bits of our tongues—they chain and hand-cuff us, and while in that miserable and wretched condition, beat us with cow-hides and clubs—they keep us half naked and starve us sometimes nearly to death under their infernal whips or lashes (which some of them shall have enough of yet)—They put on us fifty-sixes and chains, and make us work in that cruel situation, and in sickness, under lashes to support them and their families.—They keep us three or four hundred feet under ground working in their mines, night and day to dig up gold and silver to enrich them and their children.—They keep us in the most death-like ignorance by keeping us from all source of information, and call us, who are free men and next to the Angels of God, their property!!!!!! They make us fight and murder each other, many of us being ignorant, not knowing any better.—They take us, (being ignorant,) and put us as drivers one over the other, and make us afflict each other as bad as they themselves afflict us—and to crown the whole of this catalogue of cruelties, they tell us that we the (blacks) are an inferior race of beings! incapable of self government!!—We would be injurious to society and ourselves, if tyrants should loose their unjust hold on us!!! That if we were free we would not work, but would live on plunder or theft!!!! that we are the meanest and laziest set of beings in the world!!!!! That they are obliged to keep us in bondage to do us good!!!!!!—That we are satisfied to rest in slavery to them and their children!!!!!!—That we ought not to be set free in America, but ought to be sent away to Africa!!!!!!!!— That if we were set free in America, we would involve the country in a civil war, which assertion is altogether at variance with our feeling or design, for we ask them for nothing but the rights of man, viz. for them to set us free, and treat us like men, and there will be no danger, for we will love and respect them, and protect our country—but cannot conscientiously do these things until they treat us like men. ☞

How cunning slave-holders think they are!!!—How much like the king of Egypt who, after he saw plainly that God was determined to bring out his people, in spite of him and his, as powerful as they were. He was willing that Moses, Aaron and the Elders of Israel,[94] but not all the people should go and serve the Lord. But God deceived him as he will Christian Americans, unless they are very cautious how they move. What would have become of the United States of America, was it not for those among the whites, who not in words barely, but in truth and in deed, love and fear the Lord?— Our Lord and Master said:—*"[But] Whoso shall offend one of these little ones which believe in me, it were better for him that a millstone were hanged about his neck, and that he were drowned in the depth of the sea." But the Americans with this very threatening of the Lord's, not only beat his little ones among the Africans, but many of them they put to death or murder. Now the avaricious Americans, think that the Lord Jesus Christ will let them off, because his words are no more than the words of a man!!! In fact, many of them are so avaricious and ignorant, that they do not believe in our Lord and Saviour Jesus Christ. Tyrants may think they are so skillful in State affairs is the reason that the government is preserved. But I tell you, that this country would have been given up long ago, was it not for the lovers of the Lord. They are indeed, the salt of the earth. Remove the people of God among the whites, from this land of blood, and it will stand until they cleverly get out of the way.

I adopt the language of the Rev. Mr. S. E. Cornish,[95] of New York, editor of the Rights of All,[96] and say: "Any

*See St. Matthew's Gospel, chap. xviii. 6.

coloured man of common intelligence, who gives his countenance and influence to that colony, further than its missionary object and interest extend, should be considered as a traitor to his brethren, and discarded by every respectable man of colour. And every member of that society, however pure his motive, whatever may be his religious character and moral worth, should in his efforts to remove the coloured population from their rightful soil, the land of their birth and nativity, be considered as acting gratuitously unrighteous and cruel."

Let me make an appeal brethren, to your hearts, for your cordial co-operation in the circulation of "The Rights of All," among us. The utility of such a vehicle conducted, cannot be estimated. I hope that the well informed among us, may see the absolute necessity of their co-operation in its universal spread among us. If we should let it go down, never let us undertake any thing of the kind again, but give up at once and say that we are really so ignorant and wretched that we cannot do any thing at all!!—As far as I have seen the writings of its editor, I believe he is not seeking to fill his pockets with money, but has the welfare of his brethren truly at heart. Such men, brethren, ought to be supported by us.

But to return to the colonizing trick. It will be well for me to notice here at once, that I do not mean indiscriminately to condemn all the members and advocates of this scheme, for I believe that there are some friends to the sons of Africa, who are laboring for our salvation, not in words only but in truth and in deed, who have been drawn into this plan— Some, more by persuasion than any thing else; while others, with humane feelings and lively zeal for our good, seeing how much we suffer from the afflictions poured upon us by unmerciful tyrants, are willing to enroll their names in any thing which they think has for its ultimate end our redemption from wretchedness and miseries; such men, with a heart truly overflowing with gratitude for their past services and zeal in our cause, I humbly beg to examine this plot minutely, and see if the end which they have in view will be completely consummated by such a course of procedure. Our friends who have been imperceptibly drawn into this

plot I view with tenderness, and would not for the world injure their feelings, and I have only to hope for the future,
that they will withdraw themselves from it;—for I declare to
them, that the plot is not for the glory of God, but on the
contrary the perpetuation of slavery in this country, which
will ruin them and the country forever, unless something is
immediately done.

Do the colonizationists think to send us off without first
being reconciled to us? Do they think to bundle us up like
brutes and send us off, as they did our brethren of the State
of Ohio?* Have they not to be reconciled to us, or reconcile
us to them, for the cruelties with which they have afflicted
our fathers and us? Methinks colonizationists think they
have a set of brutes to deal with, sure enough. Do they think
to drive us from our country and homes, after having enriched it with our blood and tears, and keep back millions
of our dear brethren, sunk in the most barbarous wretchedness, to dig up gold and silver for them and their children?
Surely, the Americans must think that we are brutes, as some
of them have represented us to be. They think that we do
not feel for our brethren, whom they are murdering by the
inches, but they are dreadfully deceived. I acknowledge that
there are some deceitful and hypocritical wretches among
us, who will tell us one thing while they mean another, and
thus they go on aiding our enemies to oppress themselves
and us. But I declare this day before my Lord and Master,
that I believe there are some true-hearted sons of Africa, in
this land of oppression, but pretended *liberty!!!!!*—who do
in reality feel for their suffering brethren, who are held in
bondage by tyrants. Some of the advocates of this cunningly

---

*The great slave holder, Mr. John Randolph, of Virginia, intimated in
one of his *great, happy* and *eloquent* HARRANGUES, before the Virginia Convention, that Ohio is a slave State, by ranking it among other Slave-holding
States.[97] This probably was done by the HONORABLE *Slave-holder* to deter
the minds of the ignorant; to such I would say, that Ohio always was and is
now a free State, that it never was and I do not believe it ever will be a slave-
holding State; the people I believe, though some of them are hard hearted
enough, detest Slavery too much to admit an evil into their bosom, which
gnaws into the very vitals, and sinews of those who are now in possession
of it.

devised plot of Satan represent us to be the greatest set of cut-throats in the world, as though God wants us to take his work out of his hand before he is ready. Does not vengeance belong to the Lord? Is he not able to repay the Americans for their cruelties, with which they have afflicted Africa's sons and daughters, without our interference, unless we are ordered? It is surprising to think that the Americans, having the Bible in their hands, do not believe it. Are not the hearts of all men in the hands of the God of battles? And does he not suffer some, in consequence of cruelties, to go on until they are irrecoverably lost? Now, what can be more aggravating, than for the Americans, after having treated us so bad, to hold us up to the world as such great throat-cutters? It appears to me as though they are resolved to assail us with every species of affliction that their ingenuity can invent. ☞ See the African Repository and Colonial Journal,[98] from its commencement to the present day—see how we are through the medium of that periodical, abused and held up by the Americans, as the greatest nuisance to society, and throat-cutters in the world.) But the Lord sees their actions. Americans! notwithstanding you have and do continue to treat us more cruel than any heathen nation ever did a people it had subjected to the same condition that you have us. Now let us reason—I mean you of the United States, whom I believe God designs to save from destruction, if you will hear. For I declare to you, whether you believe it or not, that there are some on the continent of America, who will never be able to repent. God will surely destroy them, to show you his disapprobation of the murders they and you have inflicted on us. I say, let us reason; had you not better take our body, while you have it in your power, and while we are yet ignorant and wretched, not knowing but a little, give us education, and teach us the pure religion of our Lord and Master, which is calculated to make the lion lay down in peace with the lamb, and which millions of you have beaten us nearly to death for trying to obtain since we have been among you, and thus at once, gain our affection while we are ignorant? Remember Americans, that we must and shall be free and enlightened as you are, will you wait until we shall, under God, obtain our liberty by the crushing arm of power?

Will it not be dreadful for you? I speak Americans for your good. We must and shall be free I say, in spite of you. You may do your best to keep us in wretchedness and misery, to enrich you and your children; but God will deliver us from under you. And wo, wo, will be to you if we have to obtain our freedom by fighting. Throw away your fears and prejudices then, and enlighten us and treat us like men, and we will like you more than we do now hate you,* and tell us now no more about colonization, for America is as much our country, as it is yours.—Treat us like men, and there is no danger but we will all live in peace and happiness together. For we are not like you, hard hearted, unmerciful, and unforgiving. What a happy country this will be, if the whites will listen. What nation under heaven, will be able to do any thing with us, unless God gives us up into its hand? But Americans, I declare to you, while you keep us and our children in bondage, and treat us like brutes, to make us support you and your families, we cannot be your friends. You do not look for it, do you? Treat us then like men, and we will be your friends. And there is not a doubt in my mind, but that the whole of the past will be sunk into oblivion, and we yet, under God, will become a united and happy people. The whites may say it is impossible, but remember that nothing is impossible with God.

The Americans may say or do as they please, but they have to raise us from the condition of brutes to that of respectable men, and to make a national acknowledgement to us for the wrongs they have inflicted on us. As unexpected, strange, and wild as these propositions may to some appear, it is no less a fact, that unless they are complied with, the Americans of the United States, though they may for a little while escape, God will yet weigh them in a balance, and if they are not superior to other men, as they have represented themselves to be, he will give them wretchedness to their very heart's content.

And now brethren, having concluded these four Articles, I submit them, together with my Preamble, dedicated to the

---

*You are not astonished at my saying we hate you, for if we are men, we cannot but hate you, while you are treating us like dogs.

Lord, for your inspection, in language so very simple, that the most ignorant, who can read at all, may easily understand—of which you may make the best you possibly can.* Should tyrants take it into their heads to emancipate any of you, remember that your freedom is your natural right. You are men, as well as they, and instead of returning thanks to them for your freedom, return it to the Holy Ghost, who is our rightful owner. If they do not want to part with your labours, which have enriched them, let them keep you, and my word for it, that God Almighty, will break their strong band. Do you believe this, my brethren?—See my Address, delivered before the General Coloured Association of Massachusetts, which may be found in Freedom's Journal, for Dec. 20, 1828.[99]—See the last clause of that Address. Whether you believe it or not, I tell you that God will dash tyrants, in combination with devils, into atoms, and will bring you out from your wretchedness and miseries under these *Christian People!!!!!!*

Those philanthropists and lovers of the human family, who have volunteered their services for our redemption from wretchedness, have a high claim on our gratitude, and we should always view them as our greatest earthly benefactors.

If any are anxious to ascertain who I am, know the world, that I am one of the oppressed, degraded and wretched sons

---

*Some of my brethren, who are sensible, do not take an interest in enlightening the minds of our more ignorant brethren respecting this Book, and in reading it to them, just as though they will not have either to stand or fall by what is written in this book. Do they believe that I would be so foolish as to put out a book of this kind without strict—ah! very strict commandments of the Lord?—Surely the blacks and whites must think that I am ignorant enough.—Do they think that I would have the audacious wickedness to take the name of my God in vain?

Notice, I said in the concluding clause of Article 3—I call God, I call Angels, I call men to witness, that the destruction of the Americans is at hand, and will be speedily consummated unless they repent. Now I wonder if the world think that I would take the name of God in this way in vain? What do they think I take God to be? Do they suppose that I would trifle with that God who will not have his Holy name taken in vain?—He will show you and the world, in due time, whether this book is for his glory, or written by me through envy to the whites, as some have represented.

of Africa, rendered so by the avaricious and unmerciful, among the whites.—If any wish to plunge me into the wretched incapacity of a slave, or murder me for the truth, know ye, that I am in the hand of God, and at your disposal. I count my life not dear unto me, but I am ready to be offered at any moment. For what is the use of living, when in fact I am dead. But remember, Americans, that as miserable, wretched, degraded and abject as you have made us in preceding, and in this generation, to support you and your families, that some of you, (whites) on the continent of America, will yet curse the day that you ever were born. You want slaves, and want us for your slaves!!! My colour will yet, root some of you out of the very face of the earth!!!!!! You may doubt it if you please. I know that thousands will doubt—they think they have us so well secured in wretchedness, to them and their children, that it is impossible for such things to occur.* So did the antideluvians doubt Noah, until the

*Why do the Slave-holders or Tyrants of America and their advocates fight so hard to keep my brethren from receiving and reading my Book of Appeal to them?[100]—is it because they treat us so well?—Is it because we are satisfied to rest in Slavery to them and their children?—Is it because they are treating us like men, by compensating us all over this free country!! for our labours?—But why are the Americans so very fearfully terrified respecting my Book?—Why do they search vessels, &c. when entering the harbours of tyrannical States, to see if any of my Books can be found, for fear that my brethren will get them to read. Why, I thought the Americans proclaimed to the world that they are a happy, enlightened, humane and Christian people, all the inhabitants of the country enjoy equal Rights!! America is the Asylum for the oppressed of all nations!!!

Now I ask the Americans to see the fearful terror they labor under for fear that my brethren will get my Book and read it—and tell me if their declaration is true—viz, if the United States of America is a Republican Government?—Is this not the most tyrannical, unmerciful, and cruel government under Heaven—not excepting the Algerines, Turks and Arabs?[101]—I believe if any candid person would take the trouble to go through the Southern and Western sections of this country, and could have the heart to see the cruelties inflicted by these *Christians* on us, he would say, that the Algerines, Turks and Arabs treat their dogs a thousand times better than we are treated by the *Christians*.—But perhaps the Americans do their very best to keep my Brethren from receiving and reading my "Appeal" for fear they will find in it an extract which I made from their Declaration of Independence, which says, "we hold these truths to be self-evident, that all men are created equal," &c. &c. &c.—If the above are not day in which the flood came and swept them away. So did the Sodomites doubt, until Lot had got out of the city, and God rained down fire and brimstone from Heaven upon them, and burnt them up. So did the king of Egypt doubt the very existence of a God; he said, "who is the Lord, that I should let Israel go?"[102] Did he not find to his sorrow, who the Lord was, when he and all his mighty men of war, were smothered to death in the Red Sea? So did the Romans doubt, many of them were really so ignorant, that they thought the whole of mankind were made to be slaves to them; just as many of the Americans think now, of my colour. But they got dreadfully deceived. When men got their eyes opened, they made the murderers scamper. The way in which they cut their tyrannical throats, was not much inferior to the way the Romans or murderers, served them, when they held them in wretchedness and degradation under their feet. So would Christian Americans doubt, if God should send an Angel from Heaven to preach their funeral sermon. The fact is, the Christians having a name to

the causes of the alarm among the Americans, respecting my Book, I do not know what to impute it to, unless they are possessed of the same spirit with which Demetrius the Silversmith was possessed—however, that they may judge whether they are of the same avaricious and ungodly spirit with that man, I will give here an extract from the Acts of the Apostles, chapter xix,—verses 23, 24, 25, 26, 27.

"And the same time there arose no small stir about that way. For a certain *man* named Demetrius, a silversmith, which made silver shrines for Diana, brought no small gain unto the craftsmen; whom he called together with the workmen of like occupation, and said, Sirs, ye know that by this craft we have our wealth: moreover, ye see and hear, that not alone at Ephesus, but almost throughout all Asia, this Paul hath persuaded and turned away much people, saying, that they be no gods which are made with hands: so that not only this our craft is in danger to be set at nought; but also that the temple of the great goddess Diana should be despised, and her magnificence should be destroyed, whom all Asia and the world worshippeth."

I pray you Americans of North and South America, together with the whole European inhabitants of the world, (I mean Slave-holders and their advocates) to read and ponder over the above verses in your minds, and judge whether or not you are of the infernal spirit with that Heathen Demetrius, the Silversmith: In fine I beg you to read the whole chapter through carefully.

live, while they are dead, think that God will screen them on that ground.

See the hundreds and thousands of us that are thrown into the seas by Christians, and murdered by them in other ways. They cram us into their vessel holds in chains and in hand-cuffs—men, women and children, all together!! O! save us, we pray thee, thou God of Heaven and of earth, from the devouring hands of the white Christians!!!

> Oh! thou Alpha and Omega![103]
> The beginning and the end,
> Enthron'd thou art, in Heaven above,
> Surrounded by Angels there.
>
> From whence thou seest the miseries
> To which we are subject;
> The whites have murder'd us, O God!
> And kept us ignorant of thee.
>
> Not satisfied with this, my Lord!
> They throw us in the seas:
> Be pleas'd, we pray, for Jesus' sake,
> To save us from their grasp.
>
> We believe that, for thy glory's sake,
> Thou wilt deliver us;
> But that thou may'st effect these things,
> Thy glory must be sought.

In conclusion, I ask the candid and unprejudiced of the whole world, to search the pages of historians diligently, and see if the Antideluvians—the Sodomites—the Egyptians—the Babylonians[104]—the Ninevites[105]—the Carthagenians—the Persians[106]—the Macedonians[107]—the Greeks—the Romans—the Mahometans—the Jews—or devils, ever treated a set of human beings, as the white Christians of America do us, the blacks, or Africans. I also ask the attention of the world of mankind to the declaration of these very American people, of the United States.

A declaration made July 4, 1776.

It says, *"When in the course of human events, it becomes necessary for one people to dissolve the political bands which have connected them with another, and to assume among the Powers of the earth, the separate and equal station to which the laws of nature and of nature's God entitle them. A decent respect for the opinions of mankind requires, that they should declare the causes which impel them to the separation.—We hold these truths to be self evident—that all men are created equal, that they are endowed by their Creator with certain unalienable rights: that among these, are life, liberty, and the pursuit of happiness that, to secure these rights, governments are instituted among men, deriving their just powers from the consent of the governed; that when ever any form of government becomes destructive of these ends, it is the right of the people to alter or to abolish it, and to institute a new government laying its foundation on such principles, and organizing its powers in such form, as to them shall seem most likely to effect their safety and happiness. Prudence, indeed, will dictate, that governments long established should not be changed for light and transient causes; and accordingly all experience hath shewn, that mankind are more disposed to suffer, while evils are sufferable, than to right themselves by abolishing the forms to which they are accustomed. But when a long train of abuses and usurpations, pursuing invariably the same object, evinces a design to reduce them under absolute despotism, it is their right it is their duty to throw off such government, and to provide new guards for their future security." See your Declaration Americans!!! Do you understand your own language? Hear your language, proclaimed to the world, July 4th, 1776—☞"We hold these truths to be self evident—that ALL MEN ARE CREATED EQUAL!! that they *are endowed by their Creator with certain unalienable rights;* that among these are life, *liberty,* and the pursuit of happiness!!" Compare your own language above, extracted from your Declaration of Independence, with your cruelties and mur-

*See the Declaration of Independence of the United States.

ders inflicted by your cruel and unmerciful fathers and yourselves on our fathers and on us—men who have never given your fathers or you the least provocation!!!!!!

Hear your language further! ☞ "But when a long train of abuses and usurpation, pursuing invariably the same object, evinces a design to reduce them under absolute despotism, it is their *right*, it is their *duty*, to throw off such government, and to provide new guards for their future security."

Now, Americans! I ask you candidly, was your sufferings under Great Britain, one hundredth part as cruel and tyranical as you have rendered ours under you? Some of you, no doubt, believe that we will never throw off your murderous government and "provide new guards for our future security." If Satan has made you believe it, will he not deceive you?* Do the whites say, I being a black man, ought to be humble, which I readily admit? I ask them, ought they not to be as humble as I? or do they think that they can measure arms with Jehovah? Will not the Lord yet humble them? or will not these very coloured people whom they now treat worse than brutes, yet under God, humble them low down enough? Some of the whites are ignorant enough to tell us, that we ought to be submissive to them, that they may keep their feet on our throats. And if we do not submit to be beaten to death by them, we are bad creatures and of course must be damned, &c. If any man wishes to hear this doctrine openly preached to us by the American preachers, let him go into the Southern and Western sections of this country—I do not speak from hear say—what I have written, is what I have seen and heard myself. No man may think that my book is made up of conjecture—I have travelled and observed nearly the whole of those things myself, and what little I did not get by my own observation, I received from those among the whites and blacks, in whom the greatest confidence may be placed.

---

*The Lord has not taught the Americans that we will not some day or other throw off their chains and hand-cuffs, from our hands and feet, and their devilish lashes (which some of them shall have enough of yet) from off our backs.

The Americans may be as vigilant as they please, but they cannot be vigilant enough for the Lord, neither can they hide themselves, where he will not find and bring them out.

> ¹Thy presence why withdraw'st, Lord?
>   Why hid'st thou now thy face,
> When dismal times of deep distress
>   Call for thy wonted grace?
>
> ²The wicked, swell'd with lawless pride,
>   Have made the poor their prey;
> O let them fall by those designs
>   Which they for others lay.
>
> ³For straight thcy triumph, if success
>   Their thriving crimes attend;
> And sordid wretches, whom God hates,
>   Perversely they commend.
>
> ⁴To own a pow'r above themselves
>   Their haughty pride disdains;
> And, therefore, in their stubborn mind
>   No thought of God remains.
>
> ⁵Oppressive methods they pursue
>   And all their foes they slight;
> Because thy judgments, unobserv'd,
>   Are far above their sight.
>
> ⁶They fondly think their prosp'rous state
>   Shall unmolested be;
> They think their vain design shall thrive,
>   From all misfortune free.
>
> ⁷Vain and deceitful is their speech,
>   With curses fill'd, and lies;
> By which the mischief of their heart
>   They study to disguise.
>
> ⁸Near public roads they lie conceal'd
>   And all their art employ,
> The innocent and poor at once
>   To rifle and destroy.

[9]Not lions, crouching in their dens,
  Surprise their heedless prey
With greater cunning, or express
  More savage rage than they.

[10]Sometimes they act the harmless man,
  And modest looks they wear;
That so deceiv'd the poor may less
  Their sudden onset fear.

PART II.

[11]For, God, they think, no notice takes,
  Of their unrighteous deeds;
He never minds the suff'ring poor,
  Nor their oppression heeds.

[12]But thou, O Lord, at length arise,
  Stretch forth thy mighty arm,
And, by the greatness of thy pow'r,
  Defend the poor from harm.

[13]No longer let the wicked vaunt,
  And, proudly boasting, say
"Tush, God regards not what we do;
  He never will repay."—*Common Prayer Book.*

———

[1]Shall I for fear of feeble man,
The spirit's course in me restrain?
Or, undismay'd in deed and word,
Be a true witness of my Lord.

[2]Aw'd by mortal's frown, shall I
Conceal the word of God Most High!
How then before thee shall I dare
To stand, or how thy anger bear?

[3]Shall I, to soothe th' unholy throng,
Soften the truth, or smooth my tongue,
To gain earth's gilded toys or, flee
The cross endur'd, my Lord, by thee?

⁴What then is he whose scorn I dread?
Whose wrath or hate makes me afraid
A man! an heir of death! a slave
To sin! a bubble on the wave!

⁵Yea, let men rage, since thou will spread
Thy shadowing wings around my head:
Since in all pain thy tender love
Will still my sure refreshment prove.
                              Wesleys Collection. [108]

———

☞ It may not be understood, when I say my Third and last Edition, I mean to convey the idea, that there will be no more Books of this Third Edition printed, but to notify that there will be no more addition in the body of this Work, or additional Notes to this "Appeal." ☜

THE END

APPENDIX: DOCUMENTS

DAVID WALKER AND THE *APPEAL*

Document I
David Walker in Boston
Municipal Court
1828

*In February 1828, David Walker and two other dealers in used
clothing appeared before the Boston Municipal Court on the charge
of having received stolen goods. At this time, a number of black men
operated used-clothing establishments that were popular among the
numerous sailors of the port. Some of these merchants did knowingly
purchase stolen goods, but the vast majority did not. Nevertheless,
the popular assumption was that most of their wares were stolen, so
these black merchants were thus regularly harassed by the police.
Walker and his associates were all quickly acquitted of any crime
and, ironically, their appearance before the court provided a rare
opportunity for the newspaper to testify to the estimable characters
of the three men.* Boston Daily Courier, *12 February 1828.*

MUNICIPAL COURT. At the present term of this Hon.
Court, John E. Scarlet, David Walker and John Eli, were sev-
erally indicted for receiving stolen goods, knowing the same
to have been stolen. The defendants are colored men, and
kept stores in Brattle street, for the sale of second hand
clothing. The Government relied principally upon the fact,
that the articles charged in the indictment, as stolen goods,
had been purchased by the defendants at a price, far below
their value; and Col. Austin, the Attorney for the Commonwealth, having proved the articles charged in the indictment
to have been stolen, relied upon this fact, with the small

price paid by the defendants, for a verdict against the parties.

In behalf of the defendants it was clearly proved, that the sum paid by them to the seller, had been fully equal to the price usually paid to gentlemen of respectability, well known residents in the city; that they were accustomed to give early information of suspicious persons to the Police; and in fact a crowd of witnesses of the first standing in society, testified to their integrity and fairness in their dealings, and moral characters, to be envied by some of a fairer complexion. Scarlet was first tried, then Walker, and both acquitted by the Jury without hesitation—upon which, the Counsel of the Commonwealth entered a nol. pros. as to Eli. The result of these several investigations, is no otherwise important, than the establishment of the fact, that the Defendants, humble in life as they are, conduct their business in a fair and honorable manner. In the course of the trial, it came out accidentally, that these men were indicted on the representation of an officer of the city Government, who could not have been fully informed either of the suspicions against the defendants or the strict integrity of their characters.

Document II
David Walker Addresses the
Massachusetts General Colored Association
1828

The Massachusetts General Colored Association was founded in 1828 with the avowed intention of uniting and serving blacks throughout the North, not just in Boston. Walker was one of its leading members and eloquently articulated the excitement for this new organization and its goals in the following speech. Freedom's Journal, *19 December 1828.*

ADDRESS, *Delivered before the General Colored Association at Boston, by David Walker*

Mr. President,—I cannot but congratulate you, together with my brethren on this highly interesting occasion, the first semi-annual meeting of this Society. When I reflect upon the many impediments through which we have had to conduct its affairs, and see, with emotions of delight, the present degree of eminency to which it has arisen, I cannot, sir, but be of the opinion, that an invisible arm must have been stretched out on our behalf. From the very second conference, which was by us convened, to agitate the proposition respecting this society, to its final consolidation, we were by some, opposed, with an avidity and zeal, which, had it been on the opposite side, would have done great honor to themselves. And, sir, but for the undeviating, and truly patriotic exertions of those who were favorable to the formation of this institution, it might have been this day, in a yet unorganized condition. Did I say in an unorganized condition? Yea, had our opponents their way, the very notion of such an institution might have been obliterated from our minds. How strange it is, to see men of sound sense, and of tolerably good judgment, act so diametrically in opposition to their interest; but I forbear making any further comments on this subject, and return to that for which we are convened.

First, then, Mr. President, it is necessary to remark here, at once, that the primary object of this institution, is, to unite the colored population, so far, through the United States of America, as may be practicable and expedient; forming societies, opening, extending, and keeping up correspondences, and not withholding any thing which may have the least tendency to meliorate *our* miserable condition—with the restrictions, however, of not infringing on the articles of its constitution, or that of the United States of America. Now, that we are disunited, is a fact, that no one of common sense will deny; and, that the cause of which, is a powerful auxiliary in keeping us from rising to the scale of reasonable and thinking beings, none but those who delight in our degradation will attempt to contradict. Did I say those who delight in our degradation? Yea, sir, glory in keeping us ignorant and miserable, that we might be the better and the longer slaves. I was credibly informed by a gentleman of unquestionable veracity, that a slaveholder upon finding one of his young slaves with a small spelling book in his hand (not opened) fell upon and beat him almost to death, exclaiming, at the same time, to the child, you will acquire better learning than I or any of my family.

I appeal to every candid and unprejudiced mind, do not all such men glory in our miseries and degradations; and are there not millions whose chief glory centers in this horrid wickedness? Now, Mr. President, those are the very humane, philanthropic, and charitable men who proclaim to the world, that the blacks are such a poor, ignorant and degraded species of beings, that, were they set at liberty, they would die for the want of something to subsist upon, and in consequence of which, they are compelled to keep them in bondage, to do them good.

O Heaven! what will not avarice and the love of despotic sway cause men to do with their fellow creatures, when actually in their power? But, to return whence digressed; it has been asked, in what way will the *General Colored Association* (or the Institution) unite the colored population, so far, in the United States as may be practicable and expedient? to which enquiry I answer, by asking the following: Do not two hundred and eighty years [of] very intolerable sufferings teach us the actual necessity of a general among us? do we not know indeed, the horrid dilemma into which we are, and

from which, we must exert ourselves, to be extricated? Shall
we keep slumbering on, with our arms completely folded
up, exclaiming every now and then, against our miseries, yet
never do the least thing to ameliorate our condition, or that
of posterity? Shall we not, by such inactivity, leave, or [far-
ther] entail a hereditary degradation on our children, but a
little, if at all, inferior to that which our fathers, under all
their comparative disadvantages and privations, left on us?
In fine, shall we, while almost every other people under
Heaven, are making such mighty efforts to better their condition, go around from house to house, enquiring what good
associations and societies are going to do for us? Ought we
not to form ourselves into a general body, to protect, aid,
and assist each other to the utmost of our power, with the
beforementioned restrictions?

Yes, Mr. President, it is indispensably our duty to try every
scheme that we think will have a tendency to facilitate our
salvation, and leave the final result to that God, who holds
the destinies of people in the hollow of his hand, and who
ever has, and will, repay every nation according to its works.

Will any be so hardy as to say, or even to imagine, that
we are incapable of effecting any object which may have a
tendency to hasten our emancipation, in consequence of the
prevalence of ignorance and poverty among us? That the
major part of us are ignorant and poor, I am at this time
unprepared to deny.—But shall this deter us from all lawful
attempts to bring about the desired object? nay, sir, it should
rouse us to greater exertions; there ought to be a spirit of
emulation and inquiry among us, a hungering and thirsting
after religion; these are requisitions, which, if we ever be so
happy as to acquire, will fit us for all the departments of life;
and, in my humble opinion, ultimately result in rescuing us
from an oppression, unparalleled, I had almost said, in the
annals of the world.

But some may even think that our white breathren and
friends are making such mighty efforts, for the amelioration
of our condition, that we may stand as neutral spectators of
the work. That we have very good friends yea, very good,
among that body, perhaps none but a few of those who have,
ever read at all will deny; and that many of them have gone,

and will go, all lengths for our good, is evident, from the
very works of the great, the good, and the godlike Granville
Sharpe [*sic*], Wilberforce, Lundy, and the truly patriotic and
lamented Mr. Ashmun, late Colonial Agent of Liberia, who,
with a zeal which was only equalled by the goodness of his
heart has lost his life in our cause, and a host of others too
numerous to mention: a number of private gentlemen too,
who, though they say but little, are nevertheless engaged for
good. Now, all of those great, and indeed, good friends
whom God has given us I do humbly, and very gratefully
acknowledge. But, that we should co-operate with them, as
far as we are able by uniting and cultivating a spirit of friendship and of love among us, is obvious, from the very exhibi-
tion of our miseries, under which we groan.

Two millions and a half of colored people in these United
States, more than five hundred thousand of whom are about
two thirds of the way free. Now, I ask, if no more than these
last were united (which they must be, or always live as enemies) and resolved to aid and assist each other to the utmost
of their power, what mighty deeds could be done by them
for the good of our cause?

But, Mr. President, instead of a general compliance with
these requisitions, which have a natural tendency to raise us
in the estimation of the world, we see, to our sorrow, in the
very midst of us, a gang of villains, who, for the paltry sum of
fifty or a hundred dollars, will kidnap and sell into perpetual
slavery their fellow creatures! and, too, of one of their fellow
sufferers, whose miseries are a little more enhanced by the
scourges of a tyrant, would abscond from his pretended
owner, to take a little recreation, and unfortunately fall in
their way, he is gone! Brethren and fellow sufferers, I ask
you, in the name of God, and of Jesus Christ, shall we suffer
such notorious villains to rest peaceably among us? will they
not take our wives and little ones, more particularly our *little
ones,* when a convenient opportunity will admit and sell
them for money to slave holders, who will doom them to
chains, handcuffs, and even unto death? May God open our
eyes on these children of the devil and enemies of all good!

But, sir, this wickedness is scarcely more infernal than
that which was attempted a few months since, against the

government of our brethren, the Haytians, by a consummate rogue, who ought to have, long since, been *haltered,* but who, I was recently informed, is nevertheless, received into company among some of our most respectable men, with a kind of brotherly affection which ought to be shown only to a gentleman of honor.

Now, Mr. President, all such mean, and more than disgraceful actions as these, are powerful auxiliaries, which work for our destruction, and which are abhorred in the sight of God and of good men.

But, sir, I cannot but bless God for the glorious anticipation of a not very distant period, when these things which now help to degrade us still no more be practiced among the sons of Africa,—for, though this, and perhaps another, generation may not experience the promised blessings of Heaven, yet, the dejected, degraded, and now enslaved children of Africa will have, in spite of all their enemies, to take their stand among the nations of the earth. And, sir, I verily believe that God has something in reserve for us, which, when he shall have poured it out upon us, will repay us for all our suffering and miseries.

David Walker wrote this letter to Thomas Lewis, a free black in Richmond, Virginia, in December 1829, soon after the first edition of the *Appeal* had been printed in Boston. By securing the covert assistance of Lewis and other blacks and whites in the South, Walker hoped to circulate the book as widely as possible among the slaves there. For a transcription of the letter, see page 92, Document III. (Courtesy of the Virginia State Library, Richmond).

Where all Letters or advices emenating from your Hon, will mee with a hearty and greatful Reception ———— I am the Liberty Esteemed Sir, to Subscribe myself Yours Very Affectionately ——

David Walker

At No 42 Brattle St

Letter from David Walker to Thomas Lewis of Richmond (continued).

Document III
David Walker Mails the *Appeal* to Virginia
1829

After having published the first edition of the Appeal *in late September 1829, Walker soon sought individuals to distribute it covertly in the South. He relied on several sources to introduce the work into the South; the most important were sailors, overland travelers, and the U.S. Postal Service to deliver the work to individuals Walker had decided would be receptive to its message. One such individual was Thomas Lewis of Richmond, Virginia, a free black man about whom little is known. In the following letter, which is the only extant handwritten document of Walker's we have [see accompanying illustration], the author seeks to interest Thomas Lewis in circulating the pamphlet. The letter is held in the Slave and Free Negro Letterbook, Executive Papers of Governor John Floyd, Virginia State Library, Richmond.*

Mr. Thomas Lewis
Richmond Virginia

Boston Dec. 8th 1829

Esteemed Sir,—
Having written an Appeal to the Coloured Citizens of the World it is now ready to be submited for inspection, of which, I here with send you <u>30c</u> which Sir, your Hon, will be please to sell, among the Coloured people. The price of these <u>Books</u> is <u>Twelve cents pr Book</u>, —to those who can <u>pay for them</u>,—and if there are any who, cannot pay for a <u>Book</u> give them <u>Books</u> for nothing—If your Hon. should want any more of these <u>Books</u>, please to direct any communication to me at No. 42 Brattle St. where all letters or advices eminating from your Hon. will mee[t] with a hearty and greatful Reception—I assume the Liberty Esteemed Sir, to subscribe myself
Yours Very Affectionately

David Walker
at No. 42 Brattle St.

Document IV
Walker's *Appeal* Arrives in Georgia
1829

Late in December 1829, Henry Cunningham, a prominent preacher with the Savannah African Baptist church, received a package from David Walker that contained sixty copies of his Appeal. *Apparently unsolicited by Cunningham, the volatile pamphlets were promptly taken to the local police, who then alerted the mayor. Fearing that this was just one case of a much more general dissemination of the* Appeal *in Georgia and the South, the mayor wrote the following letter to George Gilmer, governor of Georgia. The letter is held in Records of Chatham County, Mayor's Letter Book, 1821–44, Georgia Historical Society, Savannah.*

Mayor Office
Savh. Decr. 26th 1829

Sir

I send by this days mail a pamphlet addressed to the negroes of which a parcel containing 60 was seized by the police a few days since. The parcel came from Boston in charge of the Steward, a white man and delivered to a negro preacher named Cunningham, who immediately returned it on ascertaining the character of its contents. As attempts to introduce into the ports of the South similar dangerous publications will no doubt be made, and there is every probability that their dissemination through the State may be effected [*sic*], I have deemed it my duty to communicate to you the facts in my possession that you may adopt such measures as you may deem necessary to detect or defeat these destructive efforts. Immediately after their seizure I sent one of the pamphlets to the Intendant of Charleston and another to the Mayor of Boston accompanied with a letter to apprize the one of the probability of similar attempts being made there, and to request of the other that the parties concerned in the publication might be properly dealt with.

It is left with your Excellency to judge whether it be necessary to appeal to the Governor of Massachusetts or not or whether any other measures may be desirable.

I have the honour to be Your Excellency's most obt
W. T. Williams Mayor

To his Excellency
Geo. M. Gilmer Governor
Milledgeville

Document V
A Plot to Circulate the *Appeal* in Richmond Uncovered
1830

While authorities in Richmond were aware that the Appeal *had surfaced in their town earlier, they were unaware of the mechanisms of its circulation. The following letter details what Governor William Giles had learned about the impressive covert ways in which the pamphlet had begun to move around the city and how those implicated in its circulation sought to disavow any connection with the* Appeal. *Similar sorts of underground networks would be used in other towns as well, and Walker doubtless counted on their serving this vital role. Governor Giles was so troubled by the appearance of the* Appeal *that, the same day he wrote this letter, he convened an extraordinary closed-door session of the General Assembly to discuss the "insurrectionary pamphlets." This letter is held in Executive Letter Book, reel 14, Virginia State Library, Richmond.*

Confidential
Executive Department
January 7th 1830

Sir,

In pursuance of the within advice of Council, I now do myself the honor of transmitting herewith, the accompanying pamphlet, with an original letter from a coloured man, who signs himself, "David Walker," addressed to "Mr Thomas Lewis," another free coloured man, late of this city.

These papers were presented to me on Friday morning last by Joseph Mayo Esq, the commonwealth's attorney for the Hustings Court of this city; accompanyed [*sic*] with the following information—that the coloured man Lewis to whom the letter was addressed, died some short time before the letter reached this place. That in consequence of that unexpected event, the bearer, another free coloured man, both of the letter, and of thirty pamphlets corresponding with the one now forwarded found himself at a loss, as to the disposition he should make of them—He finally however presented them to a gentleman of the city for advise in that respect—The gentleman recommended him to put the pamphlets in circulation without having read them; and, as he says, presuming them to be of the class of fanatical tracts upon the subject of religion, now profusely scattered through the country—That the whole of the thirty pamphlets were accordingly put into immediate circulation—That the Mayor of the city, having been informed of these facts, and of the mischievous tendencies of the contents of the pamphlets, immediately attempted to prevent their further circulation; and had so far succeeded, as to possess himself of twenty of the thirty copies forwarded to this city—On the same morning, I submitted the accompanying pamphlet and original letter to the consideration of the Executive Council; and was informally requested by its members to have another interview with Mr. Mayo for the purpose of obtaining more particular information upon the subject—In pursuance thereof, I requested the attendance of Mr. Mayo at my chamber on Monday last, where he did attend; and confirming his general statement before made, stated further; that the bearer of the letter and pamphlets when first charged with bringing them into Richmond, and putting them into circulation promptly denied having any concern in the transaction or any knowledge thereof—but in the course of his examination acknowledged the whole of the charges; and gave a more particular account of the circumstances attending the transaction—for which, I beg leave to refer the General Assembly to the Mayor and Attorney for the city of Richmond—I have many reasons for believing; that during the last year; and up to the present time, there has been an encreasing activity in circulating amongst the people of colour insurrectionary pamphlets and speeches, to an extent, which in my judgment requires the best attention of the General Assembly; and I therefore, and with the enclosed advise of the Executive Council, most respectfully present this extremely delicate and interesting subject to its consideration.

I have deemed it proper to make this communication confidential, for the purpose of leaving it to the option of the General Assembly, to examine it with open, or closed doors, according to its own discretion, after being apprised of the character of its contents.

> With great respect and esteem,
> your ob'dt serv't
> Wm. B. Giles

The Honorable Linn Banks
Speaker of the House of Delegates

Document VI
The Mayor of Boston Answers Southern Queries About Walker
1830

Anxious to gather more information on the mysterious Walker, and hopefully to check the flow of the pamphlets at its source, Mayor William Thorne Williams of Savannah and Governors Gilmer of Georgia and Giles of Virginia all wrote Harrison Gray Otis, mayor of Boston, about Walker and the arrival of the pamphlets. As Mayor Williams observed to Otis in his letter of 12 December 1829, he hoped "that enquiries may be instituted respecting the parties concerned in a transaction fraught with such dangerous consequences to the peace and even to the lives of the people of the South." Mayor Otis actually sent an associate to Walker's shop on Brattle Street to interview the merchant. The following letter summarizes the outcome of that meeting. The letter is reprinted in the Richmond Enquirer, *18 February 1830.*

Boston, Feb. 10, 1830

To the mayor of Savannah.
Sir: Indisposition has prevented an earlier reply to your favor of the 12th December. A few days before the receipt of it, *the pamphlet* had been put into my hands by one of the board of aldermen of this city, who received it from an individual, it not having been circulated here. I perused it carefully, in order to ascertain whether the writer had made himself amenable to our laws; but notwithstanding the extremely bad and inflammatory tendency of the publication, he does not seem to have violated any of these laws. *It is written by a free black man, whose true name it bears. He is a shop keeper and dealer in old clothes;* and in a conversation which I authorized a young friend of mine to hold with him, he openly avows the sentiments of the book and authorship. I also hear, that he declares his intention to be, to circulate his pamphlets by mail, at his own expense, if he cannot otherwise effect his object.

You may be assured, sir, that a disposition would not be wanting on the part of the city authorities here, to avail themselves of any lawful means, for preventing this attempt to throw fire-brands into your country. We regard it with deep disapprobation and abhorrence. But, we have no power to control the purpose of the author, and without it, we think that any public notice of him or his book, would make matters worse.

We have been determined, however, to publish a general caution to captains and others, against exposing themselves to the consequences of transporting incendiary writings into your and the other southern states.

I have the honor to be your obedient servant,

H. G. OTIS

Document VII
A Sailor Brings the *Appeal* to Charleston
1830

Walker and his associates in Boston favored the use of white sailors to introduce the Appeal *into Southern ports because they would arouse the least suspicion. John Ely, a close colleague of Walker's in Boston, successfully solicited a ship's white steward to carry the pamphlets to Savannah, and a similar method was probably used for Wilmington, North Carolina. The following court deposition illuminates the involvement of a white sailor, Edward Smith, with delivering the* Appeal *to Charleston. Smith, who was fined $1,000 and sentenced to one year of hard labor in prison, disavowed throughout his trial any knowledge of the contents of the pamphlet or any intent to foment insurrection. The complete text of the deposition is located in William and Jane Pease, eds., "Walker's* Appeal Comes to Charleston: A Note and Documents," *Journal of Negro History 59 (July 1974), 287–92.*

Testimony and Confession:

Information having been rec'd by the Intendant of Charleston that a white man named Edward Smith, a Steward on board of a vessel called the Columbo recently arrived from Boston, had been Engaged in distributing some pamphlets of a very seditious & inflammatory character among the Slaves & persons of color of said City, a plan was laid for his detection and apprehension which succeeded. The Captain of the Guard by posting himself in a convenient situation for the purpose, overheard a conversation between the Said Edward Smith and a negro fellow in relation to Said Pamphlets which confirmed the Statement made to the Intendant & induced Capt'n Wesner immediately to arrest said Smith & take him to the Guard House where the Guard Committee were convened to investigate the matter. This was on the Evening of Saturday the 27th of March 1830 & the following is the testimony adduced on the occasion[:]

The Captain stated that the negro in the conversation above alluded to requested Smith to give him one of the Books which he had been distributing among the negroes. Smith replied that he had none left, that he had only brought out six and had given them all away. The negro then asked if he could get any more. Smith replied that he could if he went back, that those were given to him by a decent looking black man whom he believed to be a Bookseller & that he required of him that he Should give them secretly to the Black people[,] that they had some other conversation together, but that it was very much a repetition of what had been before said. One of the pamphlets in question which had been given by the negro conveying the information to the Intendant, being shewn to Smith, he said if that was the cause of his apprehension he would tell all about it & then proceeded as follows—

That the day before he left Boston, a colored man of decent appearance & very genteely dressed called on board of the vessel and asked him if he would do a favor for him. Wit[ness] replied he would if it would not bring him in trouble. The man then said that he wished him (Smith) to bring a package of pamphlets to Charleston for him and to give them to any negroes he had a mind to, or that he met, that he must do it privately and not let any white person know any thing about it. That he Wit[ness] consented & promised the man that he would do as directed. That nothing further took place between the Said man & himself, that he did not know the man who gave him the Pamphlets, that he did not know or Enquire what the pamphlets were about, but that during the passage he one day opened one of them & read a few lines when he was called away & did not look into it afterwards—(he pointed out the part of the Pamphlet which he so read. . . . From what he read he found out *that it was something in regard to the imposition upon negroes,* that when he arrived in Charleston he would not on this account have delivered the Books, if he had not pledged his word to the Boston man to do so. That after the arrival of the vessel & when the negroes came on board to discharge the Cargo, being anxious to get rid of said Pamphlets, he asked one of the negroes, if he did not want a Book or if he would have a Book & upon the Negroes' replying in the affirmative he gave him one of said Pamphlets, that other negroes on board then applied to him & he gave away all that he had which were only *three* in number, that one of them was bran[d] new, another somewhat worn & the third had no cover upon it, *that the one now produced was one of the books which he had so distributed and the very one of which he had read a part on the passage,* that when he gave the books to the negroes he told them that he got them from a person in Boston, who, from his appearance, he thought was a minister. When he delivered them, the Captain & Mate were on board, but he does not know whether Either of them saw him deliver the books or heard what he said to the negroes, that during the voyage he kept the Said books at the head of his berth & when he was called away while reading one of them as above mentioned he threw it into his berth. He did not know that he was doing wrong or violating the law in distributing said books. He would know the negroes to whom he gave the books if he were again to see them. A short time after his arrival, a colored Cook or Steward was one day taken from a vessel lying near the Columbo, a black man near observed "there goes another one" to which Wit[-ness] replied that it was a great Shame as it turned Every thing into Confusion on board the vessel, that the negro then rejoined that that was not half. The present is the fourth time he has been in Charleston, the third time he came, he arrived on the 22 Nov'r last & remained until the Ensuing February, that he used to come ashore at night & sometimes go to the Theatre, the first & second times he came to Charleton [*sic*] he did not go ashore Except to and from the Market with the Captain. He does not know why he mentioned to the negro he conversed with that he had brought six of the Pamphlets with him, he brought but three.

The above is the testimony as correctly as it could be taken down. The confession of Smith was perfectly voluntary, neither the hope of reward nor the fear of punishment was held out to him as an inducement to make it. He had not been told by Capt'n Wesner that he had been arrested for circulating these pamphlets & the first intimation he had of the cause of his apprehension was when the book was produced to him & he was asked what he had done with the other five which he had said he brought with him & distributed. His reply to this Enquiry was that if that was what he had been taken up for he would tell all about it and then went on to relate what has been above stated. He denied that he received any reward or promise of reward from the man who gave him the pamphlets and said he was to get no good from distributing them & only did it because he had pledged his word to that purpose.

The foregoing testimony & statements were made in the presence of the Intendant, Mess'rs Yates, Waring & Shand & Capt'n Wesner.

Peter J. Shand
Chairman Guard Comm'ee
[March 27, 1830]

Document VIII
Walker's *Appeal* Alarms North Carolina
1830

Walker realized the greatest scale of the Appeal's *circulation in his home state of North Carolina. The pamphlet appears not to have arrived in the state before August 1830, entering there through the port of Wilmington as the letter below describes. As many as two hundred copies of the* Appeal *were received by Jacob Cowan, a local slave who was allowed to keep some sort of tavern and who disseminated a number of copies before he was apprehended. Local authorities were especially anxious about its arrival because rumors were currently circulating there and elsewhere in the South about some imminent emancipation, perhaps fueled by the slaves' awareness of mounting antislavery agitation in England for emancipation in its Caribbean colonies, and which would in fact begin being implemented by 1832. Slave rebelliousness had long been present along coastal North Carolina, and over the coming months the numerous black runaways populating the coastal counties would move the* Appeal *from Wilmington to Elizabeth City in the northeastern corner of the state. A friend of Walker's in Boston in early 1831 claimed that the* Appeal *was responsible for a slave uprising at New Bern in December in which sixty slaves lost their lives. The letter is held in Governor John Owen, Letterbook, 1828–30, vol. 28, North Carolina State Archives, Raleigh.*

Wilmington, N.C. August 7th, 1830

To His Excy. John Owen
Governor of State of N.C.
Dear Sir:

A few days since a well disposed free person of Color put into the hands of the commissioners of this town a pamphlet published by one David Walker of Boston, treating in most inflammatory terms of the condition of the slaves in the Southern states, exaggerating their sufferings, magnifying their physical strength and underating the power of the whites; containing also an open appeal to their natural love of liberty; and throughout expressing sentiments totally subversive of all subordination in our slaves; and inculcating principles wholly at variance with the existing relation between the two colours of our Southern population. An investigation of the affair has shewn, that the author had an Agent in this place (a slave) who had received this book with instructions to distribute them throughout the State particularly in Newbern, Fayette, & Elizabeth. The agent for the distribution of this seditious book is now in jail, and although he confesses himself the Agent, & acknowledges having received the above instructions, denies having obeyed them, and keeps (us) ignorant of the extent to which the books may have circulated:—The above circumstance taken in connection with a fact recently brought to light, viz. that a very general and extensive impression has been made on the minds of the negroes in this vicinity that measures have been taken towards their emancipation on a certain & not distant day has excited no little uneasiness in our community. And the aggregate of facts brought to light in the course of sundry police investigations of the subject satisfies most of us that a certain number of free negroes with a few slaves have for months past frequently discussed the subject of a conspiracy to effect the emancipation of the slaves in this place.

Every means which the existing laws of our State place within the reach of the police of this place are promptly used to prevent the dissemination of Walker's pamphlet, and to restore confidence to our fellow citizens. And I have felt it my duty as Chairman of this board to submit to your Excellency the above account, and likewise to submit to you the propriety & manner of making known such facts, as relate to this incendiary pamphlet, to the local authorities throughout the State, that they may be on their guard against the introduction & distribution of this book, the mischievous tendency of which is obvious to everyone, and the design of which cannot be mistaken. I would not have troubled your Exlcy with this matter, but that the circumstance, and similar occurrences which have recently been noticed in Louisiana, Georgia & South Carolina prove beyond a doubt that a systematic attempt is making by some reckless persons at the North to sow sedition among the slaves at the South, and that this pamphlet is intended & well-calculated to prepare the minds of the slave population for any measure, however desperate, that they may propose for accomplishing their emancipation. And unless some measures are taken to counteract this design in time, I fear the consequences may be serious in the extreme.

Very respectfully
Yr. Obd. Svt
James F. McKee

                    Mag. of Police. Wilmington

Document IX
Benjamin Lundy Reviews Walker's *Appeal*
1830

Benjamin Lundy, Quaker editor of the antislavery Genius of Universal Emancipation, *was one of a few people who wrote a review of the* Appeal. *Dedicated to nonviolence and moral suasion, Lundy condemned the pamphlet as an "attempt to rouse the worst passions of human nature, and inflame the minds of those to whom it is addressed." He feared that the impassioned language of Walker would lead only to black violence, which would in turn bring down horrible white reprisals and the possible "extermination of the colored race." While fully acknowledging that black Americans had "much cause for complaint," he was certain that the* Appeal *could only worsen their plight. In a January 1831 issue of the antislavery* Liberator, *another reviewer questioned whether the* Appeal *had even been written by David Walker, because he assumed no black person could evince such a level of learning, even though William Lloyd Garrison, editor of the newspaper, observed in the same issue that Walker "was hurtfully indefatigable in his studies." Lundy's review is printed in the* Genius of Universal Emancipation, *April 1830.*

WALKER'S BOSTON PAMPHLET

I had not seen this far-famed production until within a few days. A more bold, daring, inflammatory publication, perhaps, never issued from the press, in any country. I can do no less than set the broadest seal of condemnation upon it. Such things can have no other earthly effect than to injure our cause. The writer indulges himself in the wildest strain of reckless fanaticism. He makes a great parade of technical phraseology, purporting to be religious, but religion has nothing at all to do with it. It is a labored attempt to rouse the worst passions of human nature, and inflame the minds of those to whom it is addressed.

Granting that the colored race have as much cause for complaint as the writer intimates, (and I readily grant it,) yet this is not the way to obtain redress for their wrongs. The moral, not the physical, power of this nation must be put in requisition. Any attempt to obtain their liberty and just rights, by force, must for a long time to come end in defeat, if not the extermination of the colored people. It is to avert so direful a catastrophe, that the wise and the good are now exerting themselves, in various parts of our country. How painful, then, must it be to such to witness a fiery ebullition of rage, like that under consideration when every appeal should be made to reason and the judgment, instead of the malignant passions. There can be no impropriety in an expression of sentiment, on the part of the colored people, relative to their wrongs, provided it be done in a truly Christian spirit: but acrimonious language should not be indulged, and even revengeful feelings should be repressed, so much as possible. A disposition to promote turbulent and violent commotion, will only tend to procrastinate the march of justice and defer the enfranchisement of the colored race among us; of course every appearance thereof should be discountenanced by persons of every color and condition. And I am glad to find that some of the coloured people have *publicly* condemned the pamphlet in question.

Document X
A Boston Newspaper Highlights the Local Black Response to the *Appeal*
1830

The response to the Appeal *in the North is usually overlooked in favor of the far greater controversy it generated in the South. Yet as the following editorial reveals, blacks in Boston and elsewhere in the North reacted enthusiastically to it, glorying "in its principles, as if it were a star in the east, guiding them to freedom and emancipation." Walker's eloquent outrage at the brutal racism and violence black Americans confronted spoke vehemently to them wherever they lived—North or South. In Middletown, Connecticut, not far from New Haven and Hartford, the Reverend Amos Beman, a prominent black abolitionist, remembered how members of his community would gather to hear the* Appeal *and other antislavery works "read and re-read until their words were stamped in letters of fire upon our soul." Ironically, the following editorial uses their high regard for the* Appeal *as an opportunity to ask them why they are not more satisfied with what they currently have and why they are not more dedicated to raising themselves up to "the virtues of the white man." Editorial printed in the* Boston Evening Transcript, *28 September 1830.*

OUR COLORED POPULATION—There is no race of men for whom we feel more sympathy than for the poor degraded children of Africa; but we have no bowels of compassion for the contumely which they bring upon themselves by their disreputable conduct, or by their over freedom of action. Since the publication of that flagitious pamphlet, Walker's Appeal, for the consequences of which, if we mistake not, some fanatical white man will have to answer, we have noticed a marked difference in the deportment of our colored population. It is evident they have read this pamphlet, nay, *we know* that the larger portion of them have read it, or *heard* it read, and that they glory in its principles, as if it were a star in the east, guiding them to freedom and emancipation.

Freedom and emancipation! why, what do our blacks require more than they already enjoy; if the constitution of the state refuses to admit them to places of emolument and trust, are they not more than doubly compensated by not being required to perform militia service? Are they not protected in property and person as sacredly as the white man? are not our Halls of Justice as free to them as to us? It would seem as if these things were not so. It would be made to appear, that the free colored population of the Northern States actually suffered at this moment the hardships imposed upon their less favored brethren of the South. The cause of all this may be found in the untimely interference of certain very good people, who are most philanthropically busy in curing small evils, but cannot or will not see the terrible consequences that sometimes ensue from their injudicious interference.

It is not that we do not treat the colored man well, but that he has been treated too well, both for his own interest and that of the community.—He has been made too much of, and taught to "think of himself more highly than he ought to think." His good qualities are over-estimated, and his vices palliated and excused, on the score of the oppression still borne by his nation. It is quite time that his character should be studied;—that he should be led to study it himself; that he should be made acquainted with his own deficiencies, taught self-respect, educated in the virtues of the white man, and not left to the imitation of his vices.

EDITOR'S NOTES
TO WALKER'S *APPEAL*

1. Walker here refers to Pharaoh Ramses II, who ruled Egypt during the time of Moses and brutally subjugated Israel.

2. Walker refers to the bitter experience of the nation of Israel, the Jews, in ancient Egypt. The initial benevolent offer of Pharaoh, through Joseph, to allow Jacob and his progeny to settle in Egypt in the land of Goshen had, by the time of Moses three centuries later, been transformed into brutal enslavement. As recounted in the Book of Exodus, Moses led the Jews out of their bondage in Egypt.

3. The Helots were a servile population in Sparta, and other classical Greek states, who were enslaved collectively as a national group. While not owned privately by individuals like chattel slaves, they were owned by the community as a whole. The community's governing body held the right to manumit them, which it did only rarely. The principal function of the Helots was to produce a quota of essential agricultural products for the community. Treated brutally everywhere, in Sparta and other states, the Helots revolted in the seventh, fifth, and fourth centuries B.C. *The Oxford Classical Dictionary*, ed. Simon Hornblower and Anthony Spawforth, 3rd ed. (New York: Oxford University Press, 1996), 680.

4. Classical Rome was a thoroughgoing slave society where owners exercised complete dominion over the slave, including the power of life and death. At the close of the republic in 30 B.C., approximately two million slaves were held in Italy alone—25 percent of the total population. Like the Greeks, Romans usually avoided enslaving fellow compatriots, preferring instead to secure slaves from war captives, piracy, kidnapping, and the offspring of female slaves, whose status all their progeny followed. Although the rich were the largest slaveholders, many others of lesser means owned slaves as well, such as free urban artisans who often worked closely with their slaves. Slaves commonly worked at all levels of Roman life, except in public office, and not infrequently purchased their freedom, after which in Rome they might become citizens. Roman slavery, however, was a brutal institution, especially in the mines and in the large agricultural estates in southern Italy, where the great rebel, Spartacus, led a slave revolt (73–71 B.C.) that at one point numbered 120,000 rebels. *Oxford Classical Dictionary*, 1415–17, 1433.

5. Flavius Josephus (37/38–?) a Jew of Greek descent, wrote *The Jew-*

ish War, about the numerous revolts of the Jews against Roman rule since the Maccabean Revolt in 167 B.C. Despite his devotion to Judaism, Josephus in his later years defended Roman policies and was granted Roman citizenship. *Oxford Classical Dictionary,* 798–99.

6. Plutarch (c. 50–c. 120) was a great Roman essayist, philosopher, and biographer. He is best known for his *Parallel Lives*—commonly called Plutarch's *Lives*—which extolled the virtues of such leaders as Alexander the Great and Marc Antony. *Oxford Classical Dictionary,* 1200–1201.

7. Walker here is probably referring both to civil conflicts occurring in Spain and Portugal in the early decades of the nineteenth century and to those countries' loss of their slaveholding colonies in South America during the 1810s and 1820s. Following the Napoleonic Wars in early-nineteenth-century Europe, during which Napoleon's army waged a bloody occupation of Spain and Portugal, reactionary monarchs were restored to their thrones in the two countries, and others, by the conservative mandates of the Congress of Europe in 1815. The repressive Ferdinand VII of Spain soon encountered difficulties with liberals and student revolutionaries in that country, and in 1823 a large army led by France quelled rebelliousness and secured his rule. Moreover, Spain by 1824 had lost all of its South American colonies as the revolutionary republicans Simón Bolívar and José de San Martín led armies throughout the continent to destroy the remnants of Spanish rule, establish independent nations, and set in motion the abolition of slavery. After 1815 the Portuguese parliament attempted to reestablish control over Brazil, to which the royal family had fled when Napoleon occupied Portugal. But under the leadership of Pedro I, the son of King John VI of Portugal, Brazil refused to submit to parliament and declared its independence in 1822. Brazil, however, did not free its slaves. There was, finally, little the mother countries could do in the face of these dramatic events, for both Britain and the United States were, for a variety of reasons, interested in protecting these fledgling nations from any European intervention. By 1829, disruptive political struggles and military conflicts continued in the new nations of South America, and a weakening slavery persisted in Peru, Venezuela, and Bolivia. Robin Blackburn, *The Overthrow of Colonial Slavery, 1776–1848* (London: Verso, 1988), 331–417.

8. A reference to the closing of the Red Sea on Pharaoh Ramses II and his Egyptian soldiers as they pursued the fleeing Israelites, for whom God had opened a passage in the sea. Exodus 14:21–15:21.

9. A reference to the Helots held as slaves in Sparta. Lacedemon was the official name of Sparta.

10. Lycurgus (c. 650 B.C.) has traditionally been designated the founder of Sparta's austere, communal, and militaristic polity credited with making Sparta a great power in the Peloponnesian Peninsula. Although Lycurgus is enshrined in Plutarch's *Life of Lycurgus,* it is not clear whether Lycurgus ever lived. *Oxford Classical Dictionary,* 897; *The Oxford History of the Classical World,* ed. John Boardman, Jasper Griffin, and Oswyn Murray (New York: Oxford University Press, 1988), 26–27, 36.

11. Lucius Cornelius Sulla Felix (c. 138 B.C.–78 B.C.) was a great Roman general credited with the conquest of Greece and other states in

the East. Once he returned in 83 B.C. from these triumphs with his armies, he launched an attack on Rome and other key locations in Italy, soon seizing the capital and declaring himself dictator. He was infamous for ruthlessly murdering opponents and bribing friends, but in 80 B.C. he voluntarily resigned from his rule. *Oxford Classical Dictionary*, 400–401; *Oxford History of the Classical World*, 459–63.

12. Sergius Catalina (c. 108 B.C.–62 B.C.), a lieutenant of Sulla and later governor of Roman provinces in Africa, organized a conspiracy by disaffected aristocrats and war veterans against Rome in 63 B.C. However, the vigilance and eloquence of Cicero, then consul of Rome, rallied the Senate and the plot was quashed late in the year 63. *Oxford Classical Dictionary*, 1393.

13. On the Ides of March 44 B.C., as apparently foretold by an augur, Caius Julius Caesar (100 B.C.–44 B.C.), general, statesman, and writer, was assassinated in the Roman Senate by a number of senators led by Cassius and Brutus, all of whom feared Caesar's mounting power and widespread popularity with the people. Great mourning followed his death. After fleeing Rome, Cassius and Brutus were defeated in battles at Philippi by early 42, and both committed suicide. *Oxford Classical Dictionary*, 780–82; *Oxford History of the Classical World*, 467–77.

14. Antonius Marcus (82 B.C.–30 B.C.), general and ally of Julius Caesar, defeated the forces of Cassius and Brutus at Philippi by early 42 B.C. after forming a triumvirate with Aemilius Lepidus (?–13/12 B.C.) and Octavius (63 B.C.–A.D. 14)—who would become Augustus, the first emperor of imperial Rome. Marc Antony was given the lucrative rule over Rome's eastern provinces as his prize, and he soon settled in Alexandria with Cleopatra. By 32 B.C. a deep rift dividing Antony and Octavius exploded in the battle of Actium in 31 B.C., where Antony was defeated. He returned to Egypt and, with Cleopatra, committed suicide in 30 B.C. as Rome annexed Egypt. *Oxford Classical Dictionary*, 115–16; *Oxford History of the Classical World*, 531–34.

15. Aemilius Lepidus (?–13/12 B.C.), general and politician, and Octavius or Augustus (63 B.C.–A.D. 14), general and first Roman emperor, formed a triumvirate with Marc Antony to rule Rome and its provinces after the assassination of Julius Caesar in 44 B.C. After the defeat of Caesar's assassins, Brutus and Cassius, at Philippi in early 42 B.C., the three men divided the rule of the empire among themselves: Octavius was given the western portions, Antony the eastern part, and Lepidus the lands of North Africa. Persisting jealousies and disagreements over the distribution flared into armed conflict between them at various times, and by 31 B.C., after Antony's defeat at the Battle of Actium, Octavius became the sole ruler of the Roman Empire. *Oxford History of the Classical World*, 532–34; *Oxford Classical Dictionary*, 20, 216–18.

16. Philippi was a city in the Greek province of Macedonia at the edge of a large plain. In 42 B.C., the combined armies of Marc Antony, Aemilius Lepidus, and Octavius defeated those of Brutus and Cassius at Philippi. The city then became a Roman province. *Oxford Classical Dictionary*, 1162–63.

17. Cassius Longinus (?–42 B.C.) and Iunius Brutus (85–42 B.C.) were important military and government leaders in late republican Rome. Together in 44 B.C. they orchestrated the assassination of Caesar, whose rise to dictator troubled them. After the assassination, they fled Rome and organized large armies in the eastern provinces, then lost huge battles against Marc Antony and Octavius at Philippi in 42 B.C. Both committed suicide after the defeats. *Oxford Classical Dictionary*, 300–301, 788.

18. Tiberius Iulius (42 B.C.–A.D. 37) was the second Roman emperor after Augustus and notorious for his willingness to kill those who fell into disfavor or whom he suspected of subversion. His response to the people's widespread hatred of him was "Let them hate me, so long as they fear me." *Oxford Classical Dictionary*, 1523–24; *The New Century Handbook of Leaders of the Classical World*, ed. Catherine B. Avery (New York: Appleton-Century-Crofts, 1972), 370–75.

19. In early 1453, the expansionist Ottoman Empire, led then by Mohammed II, launched an assault on Constantinople, the capital of the collapsing Byzantine Empire and famous for its formidable walls. Mohammed II laid siege to the city beginning in February, deploying some of the largest bombardment cannons ever seen. By late May, the city's defenders were unable to block a huge breach in the wall, and the Turkish forces seized Constantinople. *The Harper Encyclopedia of Military History: From 3500 B.C. to the Present*, ed. R. Ernest Dupuy and Trevor N. Dupuy, 4th ed. (New York: Harper Collins, 1993), 476–77.

20. Walker refers to the aboriginal populations of continental North and South America who were variously displaced, enslaved, and exterminated over the course of European colonization of these continents from the 1490s through the 1820s of Walker's era.

21. Walker refers to the Greeks of the 1820s led by Alexander Ypsilanti, who were then revolting against their forced inclusion in the Ottoman Empire.

22. Ireland had long been subjugated by England, who since the sixteenth century had increased its military control of the island and had reduced the vast majority of Irish to landless tenants. By 1829, however, the Irish, under the leadership of Daniel O'Connell, were fighting successfully against the onerous restrictions placed on Catholics, the vast majority of Irish. T. W. Moody and F. X. Martin, eds., *The Course of Irish History* (Cork, Ireland: Mercier Press, 1967).

23. A reference to the centuries of proscription, persecution, and massacres endured by the Jews.

24. To which islands exactly Walker refers here is not certain but likely he is designating the numerous islands of the Pacific and thereby another racial group entitled to be free.

25. One of the oldest patriarchs of Judaism, Jacob, son of Isaac, probably lived in the sixteenth century B.C. Rachel, his wife, bore one daughter, Dinah, and twelve sons, each of whom was designated one of the twelve tribes of Israel. See Genesis 49.

26. Joseph was the favored son of Jacob who was secretly sold into slavery by his jealous brothers. Soon discerned as a gifted administrator by

his Egyptian owner, Joseph began a remarkable ascent that culminated in his becoming a viceroy to Pharaoh. Appointed to administer the kingdom's grain reserves during a famine, Joseph encountered his family, who had come to Egypt to buy grain. In the reconciliation that eventually followed, Pharaoh invited the family to settle in Goshen, where they prospered as herdsmen. See Genesis 37–50.

27. Massachusetts was the only state in the North in which an African American could serve as a juror, and by 1829 it was the only state in which blacks could vote on an equal footing with white males. In other states, burdensome restrictions or outright disfranchisement prevailed. It is thus no surprise that there were virtually no elected African American officials in the antebellum North. Leonard Curry, *The Free Black in Urban America, 1800–1850: The Shadow of the Dream* (Chicago: University of Chicago Press, 1981); Leon Litwack, *North of Slavery: The Negro in the Free States, 1790–1860* (Chicago: University of Chicago Press, 1961).

28. Most states in the North by the late 1820s had passed laws against blacks marrying whites. Massachusetts had had such a statute for a long time, but remarkably in 1843 the state legislature voted to repeal it after years of abolitionist agitation against the law. Litwack, *North of Slavery*, 16, 35, 60, 104–6.

29. Thomas Jefferson (1743–1826), statesman, author, agronomist, and third President of the United States (1801–9). In 1787, he published *Notes on the State of Virginia*, the only full-length book he ever wrote. The book richly details diverse aspects of economic, political, legal, and social life in postrevolutionary Virginia. In Query 14 of the study, Jefferson speculates whether blacks might be inferior to whites in intellectual and moral faculties.

30. Set adrift by his mother in a watertight cradle after Pharaoh decreed that all firstborn Jewish sons must be killed, Moses was discovered among reeds by Pharaoh's daughter, who adopted him and raised him as an Egyptian. As a young man, however, Moses became outraged at the Egyptians' brutal treatment of their Jewish slaves and killed an Egyptian who was beating an Israelite. Fleeing Egypt and wandering in the desert wilderness, Moses was embraced by the Midians and married Zipporah. God soon revealed himself to Moses as a burning bush, commanding him to lead Israel out of Egypt. Initially hesitant, Moses accepted the duty, returned to Egypt, challenged Pharaoh to release his Jewish slaves, and ultimately led Israel out of bondage. After many years of wandering, Moses restored Israel to the land of Canaan but was not allowed to enter it himself. Moses' story is told in the Bible in the books of Exodus, Leviticus, Numbers, and Deuteronomy.

31. Walker here refers to the Ottoman Empire, centered in Constantinople in Turkey, whose dominion over the eastern Mediterranean and the Balkans was rapidly contracting by the early nineteenth century. In the 1820s, most prominent conflict was with nationalists in Greece who sought their country's independence.

32. Sparta was located in the southern region of the Peloponnesian Peninsula. It began to rise to power in the eighth century B.C., when it

conquered neighboring Mesennia and reduced all its inhabitants to agricultural slaves or helots. In the mid-seventh century B.C., mounting conflict between rich and poor Spartans led to a radical restructuring of society intended to reduce these tensions: all menial labor was to be performed by helots alone; the number of citizens, and their power, was increased; all male Spartans were to undergo an austere and rigorous communal upbringing, followed by military service and membership in a mess or military club that would become the center of their adult life. These structural changes helped reduce conflict among Spartans—but not with the helots, who revolted regularly. Sparta rose to its greatest height late in the fifth century B.C. after it defeated Athens in 404 B.C. Yet its own defeat by Thebes in 371 B.C. precipitated its steady decline. *Oxford Classical Dictionary*, 1431–33; *Encyclopedia of the Ancient Greek World*, ed. David Sacks (New York: Facts on File Publications, 1995), 230–34.

33. See Thomas Jefferson, *Notes on the State of Virginia*, ed. William Peden (New York: W. W. Norton & Co., 1972), 142.

34. Walker refers to Oliver Goldsmith, *The Grecian History, From the Earliest State, to the Death of Alexander the Great*, 6th American ed. (Philadelphia, 1818).

35. Agis was the mythical first king of Sparta, apparently reigning in the late tenth century. This date, however, precedes the subjugation of the helots. *Oxford Classical Dictionary*, 1432.

36. Jefferson, *Notes on the State of Virginia*, 142.

37. The laws of Virginia and North Carolina had made manumission easier to obtain in the immediate postrevolutionary era, but by the turn of the century the rigorous test of some exemplary act, such as informing against a slave conspiracy, had been reinstated as the sole justification for manumission. Thus, securing freedom for slaves was very difficult in these two states, and elsewhere, by the early nineteenth century. Obstacles to advancement for the blacks who were free were equally daunting. While propertied free black males in North Carolina retained the right to vote until the 1820s, elsewhere in the South free blacks were denied the ballot and faced a host of discriminatory laws and customs inhibiting their economic, juridical, and social life. Ira Berlin, *Slaves Without Masters: The Free Negro in the Antebellum South* (New York: Pantheon, 1974); Curry, *The Free Black in Urban America*; John Hope Franklin, *The Free Negro in North Carolina, 1790–1860* (Chapel Hill: University of North Carolina Press, 1943).

38. With the admission of Missouri into the Union on 10 August 1821, the number of states reached twenty-four, where it remained when the *Appeal* was published in late 1829.

39. Here Walker is probably characterizing the skin pigmentation of Asians stereotypically as some intermediate range between white and black. "Mulatto" was a term applied overwhelmingly to people of mixed African and European ancestry.

40. Here Walker refers to such organizations as the American Board of Commissioners for Foreign Missions, created by New England Congregationalists in 1810 with the intention of converting non-Christians outside the United States. By the 1820s it had sent Protestant missionaries to Asia

and to Liberia in West Africa, as well as to numerous Native American tribes, among whom the Board actually did its most extensive missionary work. Oliver Wendell Elsbree, *The Rise of the Missionary Spirit in America, 1790–1815* (Williamsport, Pa.: Williamsport Printing & Binding Co., 1928), 102–52.

41. Walker refers to the Egyptian endeavor to join the Nile River with the Red Sea by way of a canal. In 601 B.C., while battling the Babylonians, Necho II commenced this canal, but it was not finished until a century later under Persian ruler Darius I. John Baines and Jaromir Malek, *Atlas of Ancient Egypt* (New York: Facts on File Publications, 1980), 51.

42. Walker refers to the belief that black Africans were the descendants of the son of Noah, Ham, whom the patriarch cursed for having seen him drunken and naked (Genesis 9:20–27). Because one of Ham's sons, Cush, was black, traditional lore has ascribed blackness as part of the curse. But only one of Ham's sons, Canaan, was actually cursed by Noah, and he was not black. *The HarperCollins Bible Dictionary*, ed. Paul J. Achtemeier (San Francisco: Harper, 1996), 399; *The Oxford Companion to the Bible*, ed. Michael D. Coogan and Bruce M. Metzger (New York: Oxford University Press, 1993), 268.

Walker here also indicates that the Egyptians were black and that "learning" (by which he means civilization) originated among them and was eventually carried by them to Greece. He made no distinction between the Egyptians and sub-Saharan black Africans, with whom he linked Egypt—scholars then and now would have largely disagreed with him on this). By way of Greece, then, the influence of black Egypt and Africa on current European culture could be discerned. This assertion upholding the centrality of Africa to Europe's ultimate rise was of great ideological significance in the early nineteenth century and was both vehemently supported and denied by thinkers on both sides of the Atlantic then. See Martin Bernal, *Black Athena: The Afro-Asiatic Roots of Classical Civilization*, vol. 1: *The Fabrication of Ancient Greece, 1785–1985* (New Brunswick, N.J.: Rutgers University Press, 1987). See also Peter Hinks, *To Awaken My Afflicted Brethren: David Walker and the Problem of Antebellum Slave Resistance* (University Park: The Pennsylvania State University Press, 1997), 181–85.

43. Carthage was founded in the late ninth century B.C. as a Phoenician colony but soon rose in power as a key commercial port and agricultural center in the western Mediterranean vying with Rome for dominance in the region. Over the following centuries, it increased its military and naval strength and expanded territorially. Hannibal (247 B.C.–182 B.C.), general and later statesman, in 219 led a huge army of cavalry and infantry from Carthage to the southeastern coast of Spain. Marching along the coast, and rallying subject people against Rome, Hannibal's army accomplished the remarkable feat of crossing the Alps and surprising Rome with an invasion of northern Italy in 217. After brilliant victories throughout Italy and an assault on Rome itself, Hannibal appeared near victory. But by 211, Roman forces had reinforced themselves and pushed Hannibal steadily southward. By 203, confined to the extreme south of Italy, Hannibal returned to Carthage and was decisively defeated by 202. After raising an-

other fleet and army in 190, he was again defeated. He fled, and in 183 committed suicide when on the verge of capture. *Oxford Classical Dictionary*, 295–96, 665–66; *Harper Encyclopedia of Military History*, 68–79.

44. Hayti, or Haiti, was the name adopted in 1804 by the formerly enslaved rebels who after more than ten years of brutal fighting with the French and the British had won the former French sugar colony of St. Domingue for themselves. In 1829, after many years of civil disorder, a united Haiti ruled by Jean Pierre Boyer was the only independent black republic in the world. The national religion of the country formally remained Catholicism, but the vast majority of the people actually practiced one form or another of the popular folk religion, Vodun. Boyer, however, had expressed some interest in promoting Protestantism as part of the nation's reconstruction. David Nicholls, *From Dessalines to Duvalier: Race, Colour, and National Independence in Haiti* (Cambridge: Cambridge University Press, 1979), 1–76.

45. The kidnapping of free blacks and fugitives was a serious problem in the North from the earliest days of late-eighteenth-century emancipations in the North through the 1850s, especially in the cities where local blacks commonly formed ad hoc vigilance groups against such perils. The captives were usually sold into slavery or, in the case of a fugitive slave, returned for the reward. One of the most nefarious ruses of kidnappers was to get another black man to ingratiate himself with a fugitive, learn about his origins, and then lure him into capture. For a vivid contemporary account of the perils Northern free blacks faced from kidnapping, see Jesse Torrey, *American Slave Trade; or, An Account of the Manner in which the Slave Dealers take Free People from some of the United States of America, and carry them away, and sell them as Slaves; and of the horrible Cruelties practised in the carrying on of this most infamous Traffic* (London, 1822). See also Peter P. Hinks, " 'Frequently Plunged into Slavery': Free Blacks and Kidnapping in Antebellum Boston," *Historical Journal of Massachusetts* 20 (Winter 1992), 16–31; Carol Wilson, *The Kidnapping of Free Blacks in America, 1780–1865* (Lexington: University Press of Kentucky, 1994).

46. First published on 11 March 1784 in Boston, the *Columbian Centinel* was originally a strongly Federalist newspaper. Its last issue was published on 29 April 1840. Frank Luther Mott, *American Journalism: A History of Newspapers in the United States Through 260 Years: 1690 to 1950*, 3rd ed. (New York: Macmillan Publishing Co., 1962), 131–33.

47. All these passages quoted from Thomas Jefferson are found in his 1787 work, *Notes on the State of Virginia*, 143. Note that instead of "genius" Jefferson actually wrote "genus." Walker also introduced into his quotation italics and small capital letters that were absent from Jefferson's published text, and omitted some commas that were in the original.

48. Walker refers to American grammarian Lindley Murray (1745–1826), who in 1795 published the first edition of his *English Grammar*. It was so popular that it was used almost exclusively in American schools through the first half of the nineteenth century and passed through numerous editions. Walker may well have used, for example, one of the following widely reproduced volumes from Murray: *English Grammar: Adapted to the*

Different Classes of Learners, with an Appendix Containing Rules and Observations, for Assisting the More Advanced Students to Write with Perspicuity and Accuracy (Hallowell, 1819); or *An Abridgement of Murray's Grammar to Which Is Added a Set of Lessons, Containing Explanations, Examples, Rules, and Questions, Suited to the Several Parts of Speech and Forms of the English Language* (Hartford, 1819). Walker likely would also have been familiar with the popular collection of readings from the English language and edited by Murray: *The English Reader; or, Pieces in Prose and Verse, from the Best Writers; Designed to Assist Young Persons to Read With Propriety and Effect; Improve Their Language and Sentiments; and to Inculcate the Most Important Principles of Piety and Virtue. With a Few Preliminary Observations on the Principles of Good Reading.* (New York, 1832). *Dictionary of American Biography* (New York: Scribner, 1990), 13:365–66 (hereafter cited as *DAB*).

49. By the late 1820s, public school systems were expanding in the urban North, but blacks were either excluded altogether or funneled into separate, inferior schools. In Boston in the 1820s, the School Committee made modest contributions to a semiprivate school for blacks named the Smith School, which had long met in the basement of the city's African Meeting House. Two other small and inferior public schools were also established for blacks. Yet when asked to build a high school for them, the School Committee refused on the grounds that blacks did not need education beyond the primary. Many black parents were very suspicious that their children learned little of value in these schools and that the School Committee was somehow complicit in this impoverished education. James and Lois Horton, *Black Bostonians: Family Life and Community Struggle in the Antebellum North* (New York: Holmes & Meier Publishers, 1979), 70–71; Stanley K. Schultz, *The Culture Factory: Boston Public Schools, 1789–1860* (New York: Oxford University Press, 1973), 157–67.

50. Parts of modern Israel and Lebanon occupy the biblical land of Canaan, where God directed the first Jewish patriarch, Abraham, to settle with his people (Genesis 12:1–7). Under Jacob, Israel moved from Canaan into the Egyptian land of Goshen (Genesis 46–47). After liberation from bondage in Egypt, Moses and Israel wandered in the desert wilderness to the east of Egypt for many years before returning to the land of Canaan, which God had promised to them.

51. Bartolomé de Las Casas (1484–1566), Franciscan friar and later Bishop of Chiapas, journeyed to the New World with many other Spanish adventurers on the fourth and last voyage of Christopher Columbus there in 1502. In 1506, he returned to Europe, studied to become a priest, and returned to the New World, where he was ordained in 1512 and served some of the leading *conquistadores* as they swept through the Caribbean subjugating the native peoples. By 1514, however, Las Casas determined that the Spaniards' brutalization of the Indians was fundamentally unchristian and began speaking out vehemently against their enslavement and for their humanity. His crusade earned him many enemies in the New World, but by 1520 he gained an audience before Charles V, who had succeeded Ferdinand to the throne of Spain in 1516. Las Casas won the new monarch over to his plea for the Indians. While Charles reformed the brutal *encomienda*

system, abuse of the natives remained widespread, and Las Casas devoted the balance of his life to defending the Indians against mistreatment, including writing the powerful book *The Devastation of the Indies*. Yet, by the 1520s Las Casas proposed using Africans imported by the Portuguese as forced labor, instead of the Indians and thereby contributed to justifying the rise of African slavery, even though he later recanted much of this initial support. Walker's assertions that Las Casas was integral to the importation of Africans into New Spain in 1503 and 1511 are wrong. Bartolomé de Las Casas, *The Devastation of the Indies: A Brief Account*, trans. Herma Briffault with an introduction by Bill M. Donovan (Baltimore: Johns Hopkins University Press, 1992).

52. Walker refers to Frederick Butler, *A Complete History of the United States of America, Embracing the Whole Period from the Discovery of North America Down to the Year 1820*, 3 vols. (Hartford, 1821). In volume 1, pp. 23–25, Butler discusses the roots of African slavery in the Spanish possessions, the role of Las Casas, and Charles V's granting of the license, or *asiento*, to a Flemish merchant to import 4,000 Africans to Spain's colonies.

53. Walker refers to the introduction of Africans into the British North American colonies. The Dutch sold "twenty Negars" to English colonists at Jamestown in August 1619, not 1620. Warren M. Billings, ed., *The Old Dominion in the Seventeenth Century: A Documentary History of Virginia, 1606–1689* (Chapel Hill: University of North Carolina Press, 1975), 155.

54. In the South there were many laws prohibiting slaves from gathering in groups of three or more, without white supervision, for any reason including worship. Local patrols usually comprising ordinary white male citizens were empowered to enforce these regulations and to punish violators summarily. After Nat Turner's religiously inspired insurrection in Southampton County, Virginia, in late August 1831, laws against independent black preachers and unsupervised religious gatherings were enforced even more vigorously.

55. Walker refers to the famous conversion of the Roman centurion Cornelius by the apostle Peter at Caesarea, described in Acts 10. Peter declared: "Truly I perceive that God shows no partiality, but in every nation any one who fears him and does what is right is acceptable to him. You know the word which he sent to Israel, preaching good news of peace by Jesus Christ (he is Lord of all)" (Acts 10:34–36).

56. Deism, a form of religious belief current in the eighteenth century, argued for God's remoteness from the world and its affairs after the act of creation, and thus downplayed a close relationship between God and individual believers. According to the Deists, God impelled the universe and endowed it with a host of unalterable natural laws that scientific inquiry would uncover. While it never gained much of a foothold in England or America, Deism was promoted successfully in eighteenth-century France by Rousseau and such famed *philosophes* as Voltaire and Diderot. James Turner, *Without God, Without Creed: The Origins of Unbelief in America* (Baltimore: Johns Hopkins University Press, 1985), 35–72.

57. Americans in the 1820s were generally enthusiastic supporters of democratic independence movements in Ireland—and especially Greece,

making laudatory speeches, sending donations, and even sometimes enlisting to fight in Greece, as New Englander Samuel Gridley Howe did. Myrtle A. Cline, *American Attitudes Toward the Greek War of Independence, 1821–1828* (Atlanta: n.p., 1930).

58. Such racially segregated seating was routine in antebellum Northern churches. Blacks were often made to sit in elevated galleries at the rear of the church or in pews with screens in front of them near the entrance to the church. Carol V. R. George, *Segregated Sabbaths: Richard Allen and the Emergence of Independent Black Churches, 1790–1840* (New York: Oxford University Press, 1973).

59. In 1826, a Freemason in upstate New York, William Morgan, was abducted and disappeared after he threatened to expose secret Masonic rituals and membership. Despite relentless efforts to investigate his disappearance, local officials offered little help and fueled a belief in a cover-up. Soon a popular groundswell against the Masons spread throughout the Northeast, amid charges that the society conspired to suppress liberty and democratic institutions and that it was anti-Christian and a haven for drunks. By 1829, the movement was becoming politicized, and anti-Masonic parties appeared in a number of Northern states, including Massachusetts, and contributed significantly to the rise of the Whig Party in the early 1830s. The anti-Masonic movement often joined forces with other social reform movements that were also gaining popularity in the North by the late 1820s. Two of the most important were the agitation for temperance led by such clerics as Boston's Lyman Beecher, and the crusade for enforcing observance of the Sabbath and refraining on that day from all business and work activities, including delivering the mail. For an excellent discussion of this process in New York, see Paul E. Johnson, *A Shopkeeper's Millennium: Society and Revivals in Rochester, New York, 1815–1837* (New York: Hill & Wang, 1978).

60. Walker here refers to the relationship that the French, Dutch, and English in the Caribbean, slaveholders and otherwise, formed with blacks. By the 1820s, the presence of the Dutch as slaveholders in the Caribbean was negligible, maintaining colonies at Curaçao and in northern South America at Surinam. The French had fought savagely to keep St. Domingue from slave rebels in the early years of the nineteenth century, but failed to recapture it. In the 1820s, however, France still had vital slave-based sugar islands at Guadeloupe, Martinique, and elsewhere in the Lesser Antilles. France would not finally outlaw slavery in its colonies until 1848. The British were by far the largest slaveholders in the Caribbean in the 1820s, with tens of thousands of slaves in Jamaica, Barbados, Demerara, and numerous smaller holdings in the Caribbean basin. Although all three of these nations had earned infamy for their brutal treatment of the slaves, Walker probably highlighted the relative benevolence of the British because that country voluntarily ended its involvement in the Atlantic slave trade in 1808, instituted measures in the 1810s to ameliorate the conditions of the slaves in its sugar colonies, and by the late 1820s had a very active and influential antislavery movement that would lead to the abolition of slavery in all British lands by 1836. In another speech, Walker specifically lauded such giants

of the British movement against the Atlantic slave trade as Granville Sharp and William Wilberforce. See *Freedom's Journal*, 19 December 1828, reprinted in the Appendix, Document II, 85–89. See also David B. Davis, *The Problem of Slavery in the Age of Revolution, 1770–1823* (Ithaca, N.Y.: Cornell University Press, 1975); Blackburn, *The Overthrow of Colonial Slavery*.

61. Walker here refers to William Watkins (1801–58), a free black of Baltimore who was a teacher, physician, and widely respected community activist. Writing under the pseudonym "The Colored Baltimorean," Watkins wrote many incisive essays attacking the American Colonization Society in the late 1820s and early 1830s, some of which appeared in *Freedom's Journal*. He has been credited with helping to persuade the leading white abolitionist, William Lloyd Garrison, to abandon the cause of colonizationism by 1830. In 1837, Watkins played a key role in founding the black-led American Moral Reform Society. Bettye J. Gardner, "William Watkins: Antebellum Black Teacher and Anti-Slavery Writer," *Negro History Bulletin* 39 (September–October 1976), 623–25; Christopher Phillips, *Freedom's Port: The African American Community of Baltimore, 1790–1860* (Urbana: University of Illinois Press, 1997), 220–24.

62. Henry Clay (1777–1852), statesman and politician, served in the federal government from 1809 until his death as congressman, Secretary of State, and senator. In the late 1820s, he was a principal architect of the Whig Party, in which he enshrined his nationalistic American System—a plan to strengthen the young nation's economy and sectional interconnections through a national bank, a protective tariff, and an expanding network of roads, canals, and ultimately railroads. Often dubbed the Great Compromiser, Clay earned the title by skillfully engineering the Compromises of 1820, 1833, and 1850. Clay was one of the founders of the American Colonization Society and one of the most vigorous proponents of its plan to resettle America's free blacks outside of the country. Throughout Article IV of the *Appeal*, Walker illuminated Clay's key involvement with the organization. Robert Remini, *Henry Clay: Statesman for the Union* (New York: W. W. Norton & Co., 1991); *DAB*, 4:173–79.

63. Elias Boudinot Caldwell (1775–1825), a lawyer and philanthropist born in Elizabethtown, New Jersey, lost his mother in 1780 and his father in 1781, both in defense of the Revolution. He and his siblings were then placed under the care of his namesake, Elias Boudinot, a noted local jurist who saw to Caldwell's graduation from Princeton. In 1801, he was admitted to the bar and began his legal career. Caldwell was also a devout Presbyterian and licensed to preach. He was involved with local Bible societies and numerous philanthropic efforts, even helping to recover some free blacks who had been kidnapped into slavery. In late 1816, with Robert Finley of Basking Ridge, New Jersey, Caldwell helped to organize the American Colonization Society and recruit many nationally prominent men to attend its inaugural meeting on 21 December 1816. He was then elected the executive secretary of the society and became one of its principal promoters in its early years. [Hallie L. Wright], "Sketch of Elias Boudinot Caldwell," *Records of the Columbia Historical Society* 24 (1922), 204–13; P. J. Staudenraus,

The African Colonization Movement, 1816–1865 (New York: Columbia University Press, 1961), 24–30.

64. One of the first newspapers published in the nation's new capital, the *National Intelligencer,* was inaugurated on 31 October 1800 and maintained a close relationship with the succession of Democratic-Republican presidents through James Monroe. By 1829 and the Jackson administration, the *National Intelligencer* was losing favor and veered toward the new Whig Party, who commanded its loyalty until the party's demise in the mid-1850s. The newspaper ceased publishing in June 1869. Mott, *American Journalism,* 176–79.

65. Walker here refers to Dr. Jesse Torrey, physician and abolitionist, who wrote *The Moral Instructor, and Guide to Virtue and Happiness. In Five Parts* (Ballston Spa, N.Y., 1819), in which is contained the essay Walker mentions here, actually entitled "Essays on the General Diffusion of Knowledge and Moral Improvement." These essays probably influenced Walker's dedication to individual moral improvement and education. Torrey also published a lengthy condemnation of the domestic slave trade and the kidnapping of free blacks in the United States: *A Portraiture of Domestic Slavery in the United States with Reflections on the Practicability of Restoring the Moral Rights of the Slave, Without Impairing the Legal Privileges of the Possessor* (Philadelphia, 1817). Walker quotes from the speeches of Henry Clay and, later, of Elias B. Caldwell, all of which are excerpted in Torrey's *Portraiture,* 85, 86.

66. Walker refers to the meeting in Washington, D.C., on 21 December 1816 inaugurating the American Colonization Society, the purpose of which was to help free blacks by removing them from the prejudice hindering their advancement in America and resettling them in some location in Africa where they could exercise greater self-determination. The initial membership included such prominent white Americans as Henry Clay, Bushrod Washington, and Francis Scott Key, and the society and its plans for black relocation became quite popular in the 1820s. All the following quoted speeches come from a report of this meeting in the *National Intelligencer,* 24 December 1816, and in Jesse Torrey, *Portraiture of Domestic Slavery,* 85, 86. Staudenraus, *The African Colonization Movement.*

67. Fowler's Garden was a popular gathering spot for large public banquets and orations in Lexington, Kentucky, in the 1820s. Henry Clay gave a major speech there on 16 May 1829, which Walker quotes in the *Appeal.* The complete text of the speech is contained in Calvin Colton, ed., *The Works of Henry Clay: Comprising His Life, Correspondence and Speeches,* vol. 7 (New York: G. P. Putnam & Sons, 1904), 369–87 (the quoted passage is found on 386–87). Remini, *Henry Clay,* 348.

68. Albert Gallatin (1761–1849), financier, diplomat, and politician, was born in Geneva, Switzerland, into an affluent family. Chafing under the restraints of his family, and influenced by the ideas of the French philosopher Rousseau, Gallatin immigrated to America in 1780. By 1784, he had settled in western Pennsylvania, where he never fared well as a farmer but did succeed politically as a supporter of Jefferson and Western agricultural interests. Elected to Congress in 1795, Gallatin remained there until 1801,

at which time the new President, Thomas Jefferson, appointed him secretary of the treasury. Holding the office until 1814, Gallatin was critical to maintaining American financial stability at a time when embargoes and wars threatened to ruin the economy. In 1813, President James Monroe sent him to Europe to negotiate a treaty with Great Britain. He also played an important role in concluding the War of 1812 with the Treaty of Ghent in December 1814. From 1815 until the end of his public career in 1827, Gallatin served in key diplomatic posts in France and England and secured favorable commercial treaties with Great Britain. *DAB*, 7:103–10.

Walker refers here and in the quoted material at the bottom of the following paragraph to Henry Clay's efforts while secretary of state during the administration of John Quincy Adams to reach an agreement with Great Britain for the return of all fugitive slaves who fled from the United States to Upper Canada. This was especially a problem for slaveholders in Kentucky, Clay's home state. See Henry Clay's letter to Albert Gallatin, U.S. Ambassador to Great Britain, 19 June 1826, in James F. Hopkins and Mary W. M. Hargreaves, eds., *The Papers of Henry Clay*, vol. 5 (Lexington: University Press of Kentucky, 1973), esp. 471–73.

69. Walker here refers to Liberia, located on the west coast of Africa just below Sierra Leone. Liberia was developed under the auspices of the American Colonization Society (ACS) in the early 1820s as a location to receive free blacks from America. The first settlers arrived in 1820, and from that time on their numbers grew, especially in the 1830s when many manumitted slaves from Virginia and Maryland moved there. While Liberia was never an official colony of the U.S. government, funding from the government was nevertheless made available to ACS agents, especially during the administrations of Presidents Monroe and Adams and in smaller amounts throughout the balance of the antebellum era. Relations between the settlers and the native tribes were often strained, and armed conflict and exploitation were not uncommon. In 1847, Liberia became an independent nation. Tom W. Shick, *Behold the Promised Land: A History of Afro-American Settler Society in Nineteenth Century Liberia* (Baltimore: Johns Hopkins University Press, 1980); Staudenraus, *The African Colonization Movement*.

70. See *National Intelligencer*, 24 December 1816.

71. Walker refers to British actor and etymologist, Thomas Sheridan (1719–88), who in 1789 published the revised edition of *A General Dictionary of the English Language*. *Dictionary of National Biography*, 18:87–88 (hereafter cited as *DNB*).

72. Solomon, son of David and Bathsheba, ruled over Israel in the tenth century B.C. His skill and wisdom as a leader were credited with consolidating Israel's rule in the region, extending its international trade routes, and enhancing the stature of Jerusalem by embarking on an elaborate building program there. *Harper Collins Bible Dictionary*, 1048–49; *Oxford Companion to the Bible*, 707–8.

73. Walker cites from Matthew 10:26–27: "So have no fear of them; for nothing is covered that will not be revealed, or hidden that will not be

known. What I tell you in the dark, utter in the light; and what you hear whispered, proclaim upon the housetops."

74. During the antebellum period, public schools were virtually non-existent in the South outside of towns and contributed to high rates of illiteracy among working-class and rural whites, especially when compared with the Northeast. North Carolina, Georgia, Virginia, and other Southern slave states had passed stern laws against educating slaves, and, in a panic when the *Appeal* appeared in their towns in late 1829 and 1830, those laws were reinforced. Clement Eaton, *The Freedom of Thought Struggle in the Old South* (New York: Harper & Row, 1964), 64–88; Clement Eaton, "A Dangerous Pamphlet in the Old South," *Journal of Southern History* 2 (August 1936), 323–34.

75. The Antediluvians (which Walker has misspelled as Antideluvians) were the people living before the flood that, according to the Bible, inundated the world during the time of Noah. See Genesis 6–8.

76. Sodom and Gomorrah were two ancient cities along the Dead Sea that were infamous for their moral wickedness, especially male homosexuality. Abraham sent his nephew, Lot, to these and other cities to forge alliances in his wars with neighboring kings. However, both cities proved incorrigible, so Lot and his family were commanded by God to leave them just before he destroyed them through immolation. See Genesis 13:14–18, 14, 18:16–33, 19:1–29. *Harper Collins Bible Dictionary*, 1046; *Oxford Companion to the Bible*, 707.

77. Walker refers to antiblack riots that had occurred in Cincinnati, Ohio, in late August 1829. Concerned about the growing number of free blacks and fugitive slaves in the city, approximately 300 whites attacked a black neighborhood, murdering one and wounding several others. Terrorized, a number of local free blacks banded together and organized a committee to foster their immigration to Canada. Curry, *The Free Black in Urban America*, 101–4; Litwack, *North of Slavery*, 72–74.

78. To what Walker refers here exactly is not clear. The following are some possible explanations. For Kentucky he is probably referring to the recapture in late 1829 of a large number of slaves who had recently escaped from a coffle there, and imminent sale into the Deep South. Two white slave traders were killed during the escape, and soon after recapture four of the slaves were executed. Walker highlights this event and its meaning for him in the *Appeal*, 25–27. Further information is supplied in *Niles' Register*, 26 December 1829. Walker's outrage at this event is discussed further in Hinks, *To Awaken My Afflicted Brethren*, 218–21. While there are many events and persons that could have to do with the reference to South Carolina, Walker is perhaps concerned here with the current efforts in South Carolina to impede the circulation of his pamphlet in Charleston and elsewhere in the state. An attack on South Carolina and similarly guarded Southern states is implicit in Walker's footnote in the *Appeal*, 73n. For further discussion of this context, see Hinks, *To Awaken My Afflicted Brethren*, 145–49. The reference to Florida is the most cryptic, but Walker here might be condemning the treatment of the Seminoles and their black allies in the interior of the state. Some of them had already removed from the

state under intense pressure from the administration of President Andrew Jackson and accepted offers to resettle on government land in the trans-Mississippi West. Jackson had earlier fought a pitched war with the Seminoles in 1815–16 in Florida in what is called the First Seminole War, and from 1835 to 1842 a second fierce struggle would be waged between federal troops and the Seminoles and blacks who refused to relocate. See Francis Paul Prucha, *The Sword of the Republic: The United States Army on the Frontier, 1783–1846* (New York: Macmillan Co., 1969), 129–34, 269–306.

79. In early 1830, Frederick Brimsley, a friend of David Walker's, was prohibited by police from occupying a pew he had purchased for his family at the Park Street Meeting House, one of Boston's most prominent houses of worship. Edward S. Abdy, *Journal of a Residence and Tour in the United States of North America, from April, 1833, to October, 1834*, 3 vols. (London, 1835), 1:133–35.

80. John Randolph of Roanoke (1773–1833), congressman and orator, was a scion of one of Virginia's most noted families. Trained in the law, Randolph had by the late 1790s become more interested in public affairs, and in 1799 he ran for Congress as a Jeffersonian and won. Thus began his long affiliation with the House of Representatives, in which he would serve consistently, save for a few brief absences, until 1829. Randolph quickly distinguished himself as a brilliant and scathing orator who repeatedly attacked any enlargement of the national government's powers, even as Republicans in Virginia and other states became more nationalist. As the debate over slavery heated up in Congress in the 1820s, Randolph became an ever fiercer defender of state's rights. Robert Dawidoff, *The Education of John Randolph* (New York: W. W. Norton & Co., 1979); *DAB*, 15:363–67.

81. While the source of this belief that the Haitians were "bound to protect and comfort us" is not certain, three reasonable possibilities do exist. Walker was of course inspired by the example of successful slave revolt in St. Domingue in the 1790s, which led to the creation of the world's first independent black republic, Haiti, in 1804. He likely assumed that the Haitians shared in the solidarity he felt with them and would therefore support the current struggles of African Americans, even though that would be dangerous for the fledgling nation, surrounded as it was by such hostile Atlantic powers as the United States, Britain, and France. Walker, who was probably in Charleston, South Carolina, as the failed Denmark Vesey conspiracy was unfolding there in the first half of 1822, may well have been influenced also by the conspirators' belief that Haiti supported their rebelliousness, and would send vessels to assist them in fighting and offer them refuge. Moreover, by the early 1820s, the new president of Haiti, Jean Pierre Boyer, was promoting emigration of free African Americans to the island through black agents, such as Prince Saunders and Thomas Paul. There, Boyer believed, these emigrants could prosper while they brought much-needed skills and enterprise to a Haiti economically devastated by decades of revolution and civil war. During this promotion, which had largely failed by 1825, Boyer had presented himself as sympathetic to the problems confronting free blacks in the United States and offered Haiti as a haven from them, although never at any time indicting the white powers

of an America from which he unsuccessfully pursued recognition. See Robert S. Starobin, ed., *Denmark Vesey: The Slave Conspiracy of 1822* (Englewood Cliffs, N.J.: Prentice-Hall, 1970), 19, 20, 22, 30, 35, 37, 39; Hinks, *To Awaken My Afflicted Brethren*, 29–40, 99–101; Julie Winch, "American Free Blacks and Emigration to Haiti, 1804–26," *Documentos de Trabajo*, Centro de Investigaciones del Caribe y America Latina, Universidad Interamericana de Puerto Rico, 33 (August 1988), 1–22.

82. Richard Allen (1760–1831), minister, bishop, and community leader, was born a slave in Philadelphia but purchased his freedom by 1786. An ardent Methodist, Allen was an itinerant preacher in the years immediately after the Revolution. Settling in Philadelphia by the mid-1780s, he soon gathered a large and devoted black congregation around him. Enduring several heated controversies with local white Methodists over the ensuing years, Allen and his flock separated altogether from them in 1816 and formed the African Methodist Episcopal Church. He was a dominant figure in black Philadelphia in the early decades of the nineteenth century and helped inaugurate the Negro Convention Movement in 1831, just before his death. George, *Segregated Sabbaths*; Gary Nash, *Forging Freedom: The Formation of Philadelphia's Black Community, 1720–1840* (Cambridge: Harvard University Press, 1988); Charles H. Wesley, *Richard Allen: Apostle of Freedom* (Washington, D.C.: Associated Publishers, 1935); *Dictionary of American Negro Biography*, 12–13 (hereafter cited as *DANB*).

83. Generally considered the first African American newspaper in the United States, *Freedom's Journal* was inaugurated on 16 March 1827 under the joint editorship of John Russwurm and Samuel Cornish. The editors ultimately became divided over the colonization issue, and the split led to the demise of the paper in 1829. David Walker was an ardent supporter of the newspaper and served as its Boston agent. Bella Gross, "*Freedom's Journal* and the *Rights of All*," *Journal of Negro History* 17 (1932), 241–86.

84. The African Methodist Episcopal Church was created in Philadelphia in 1816 by Richard Allen, who became its first bishop. It was among the first organized, exclusively black denominations, and it grew significantly in the 1820s, especially among African Americans in towns and cities in the Middle Atlantic states. George, *Segregated Sabbaths*.

85. Joseph Addison (1672–1719) was a British poet, essayist, and statesman, perhaps best remembered for his essays and literary criticism in the famous British periodical of the early eighteenth century, *The Spectator*. *DNB*, 1:122–31.

86. Walker here refers to the effort to establish an AME church in Charleston in 1817 by Morris Brown—an AME minister recently ordained by the Reverend Richard Allen—and numerous other Charleston free blacks and slaves. While they managed to secure a charter of incorporation for the church from the state legislature that year, municipal authorities were firmly opposed to it, and harassed it with various measures into the early 1820s. Nevertheless, the church remained and only seemed to grow in popularity among local blacks whose congregation may have numbered more than 4,000. Yet when authorities linked the church with the Denmark Vesey conspiracy of 1822, they seized the opportunity to close the church

once and for all, and soon after razed the building. Hinks, *To Awaken My Afflicted Brethren*, 22–40.

87. The Scribes and Pharisees are arrayed in the New Testament as obdurate opponents of Jesus Christ. Both groups were from the learned class of Jews in Jerusalem and objected to the new teachings of Jesus. Jesus' encounters with them are described in Matthew 23.

88. The Prophets were such figures from the Old Testament as Moses, Jeremiah, and Ezekiel, who had some direct personal relationship with God that allowed him to speak directly through them. They were instrumental in leading and chastising Israel and according to Christian theology in fore-telling the arrival of Jesus Christ.

89. Walker here refers to Matthew 21:12–13.

90. Noah, who built the Ark as God commanded, was the father of Shem, Ham, and Japheth. See Genesis 5:32.

91. Walker refers to God's flooding of everything on the earth except Noah, his three sons, and their four wives. After the rains ceased and the waters receded, "the ark came to rest upon the mountains of Ararat." See Genesis 7:23–8:5.

92. Cain and Abel were the first sons of Adam and Eve after their expulsion from Eden. Cain killed Abel after God accepted Abel's offering but not Cain's. God therefore marked Cain and cursed him with inability to cultivate the soil. Cain later founded the first city, Enoch. Walker refers to the common, long-held belief that an essential part of the curse God placed on Cain was blackness—thus the assertion that contemporary African Americans were "the seed of Cain" (Genesis 4:1–17).

93. Walker's figures for Jamaica are actually quite accurate. In 1834, on the eve of full emancipation in the British West Indies, Jamaica had 311,070 slaves, 16,600 whites, and 42,000 black freedmen. Obviously there were far more than six or eight blacks to every white in the slave-based sugar islands. Most of South America did not have the same high level of reliance on Africans as laborers, so black-to-white ratios would not be as high. But in much of Brazil and northeastern South American colonies, such as Dutch Surinam and English Demerara, blacks far outnumbered whites. For example, in Demerara in 1829, slaves numbered 69,465, black freedmen 6360, and all whites just 3,006. Walker's numbers for the total black population of Georgia and South Carolina exceed the actual figures a little: in 1830 the total black population of Georgia was 220,017 (45.3 percent) and of South Carolina was 323,322 (55.6 percent). He is closer for Virginia, which had 517,105 (49.5 percent) blacks in 1830. Yet Walker's claim that "there are at least three coloured persons for one white" in the South is greatly inflated. In terms of total Southern population in 1830, whites clearly outnumbered blacks. In some states with very high black populations, such as Louisiana, Mississippi, and South Carolina, blacks were the majority, but never by more than 59 percent. In certain districts of these states and others—such as the sugar parishes north of New Orleans, the cotton-growing regions of northern Mississippi and Alabama, and the rice-growing parishes of coastal Carolina and Georgia—blacks certainly might outnumber whites by 2 to 1 or even sometimes by 3 to 1, but such

regional demographic dominance by blacks did not apply to the antebellum South as a whole. B. W. Higman, *Slave Populations of the British Caribbean, 1807–1834* (Baltimore: Johns Hopkins University Press, 1984), 418, 433; Donald B. Dodd, ed., *Historical Statistics of the States of the United States: Two Centuries of the Census, 1790–1990* (Westport, Conn.: Greenwood Press, 1993).

94. Aaron, the brother of Moses, assisted Moses in the exodus from Egypt and in leading Israel to the land of Canaan, where, like Moses, he also was denied entry by God. The elders of Israel, the senior male leaders of the various tribes of Israel, were responsible for local government and the administration of justice.

95. Samuel Cornish (1795–1858), editor, minister, and abolitionist, was born of free parents in Delaware but spent most of his adult life in or around New York City. An ordained Presbyterian minister, he organized a church in the early 1820s in New York City. By 1827, he had become one of the editors of *Freedom's Journal* and would edit alone in 1829 the short-lived *Rights of All*. In the late 1830s, he helped edit the influential *Colored American*. Cornish became an ardent abolitionist in the early 1830s and participated in a number of other moral reform and missionary endeavors as well. From the late 1820s on, he was a fierce opponent of the colonization movement. *DANB*, 134–35; Jane and William Pease, "The Negro Conservative: Samuel Eli Cornish," in *Bound with Them in Chains: A Biographical History of the Antislavery Movement* (Westport, Conn.: Greenwood Press, 1971), 140–61.

96. A short-lived but influential early African American newspaper edited by Samuel Cornish, the *Rights of All* began publishing in mid-1829 immediately following the collapse of the nation's first black newspaper, *Freedom's Journal*. David Walker served as the Boston agent for the paper. By the end of the year, the new newspaper had expired. Gross, "*Freedom's Journal* and the *Rights of All*," 241–86.

97. John Randolph made numerous lengthy speeches at the Virginia Constitutional Convention of 1829–30. Some of them addressed the issue of slavery. However, the passage where Randolph designated Ohio a slave state was not located. Randolph was a key supporter of the Northwest Ordinance of 1787, which included the prohibition of slavery in Ohio. See *Proceedings and Debates of the Virginia State Convention of 1829–1830* (Richmond, 1830); Russell Kirk, *John Randolph of Roanoke: A Study in American Politics* (with selected speeches and letters) (Chicago: Henry Regnery Co., 1964), 133–34.

98. Inaugurated in March 1825, the *African Repository & Colonial Journal* was the voice of the American Colonization Society. It published a wide variety of articles about free black life in the United States and about the history and civilization of sub-Saharan Africa.

99. Also called the Massachusetts General Colored Association, the group was probably organized in 1828—or perhaps 1826—and existed until 1833. One of the first avowedly political groups formed by antebellum free blacks, it aspired to serve the interests of African Americans throughout the North, not just in Boston. The address Walker refers to here is

found in the Appendix, Document II. Hinks, *To Awaken My Afflicted Brethren*, 75–76.

100. When the *Appeal* was discovered by white authorities in the ports and towns of Virginia, North Carolina, South Carolina, Georgia, and Louisiana, it caused an immediate uproar, and officials labored to stanch its spread and retrieve the copies that had already been disseminated. In addition, existing laws against slave literacy, circulation of seditious literature, and interaction between local blacks and free black sailors entering Southern ports were strengthened. For a fuller discussion of these events, see the Introduction, xxxviii–xli. See also Hinks, *To Awaken My Afflicted Brethren*, 116–72.

101. Walker here refers to three peoples from the region of North Africa notorious for their supposed brutality to slaves and the conquered. The Turks were the leaders of the Ottoman Empire, which by the seventeenth century extended in the east from Egypt to Morocco on the western coast of North Africa. The principality west of Egypt, called the Maghreb, was organized around three capitals at Tripoli, Tunis, and Algiers, where Turkish *pashas* prevailed over the native Arab and Berber peoples. By the early eighteenth century, local Arab ruling families had gained much greater influence over the *pashas* and the respective capitals and their hinterlands. Their principal sources of revenue by then, however, were raids on commercial shipping in the Mediterranean—seizing the cargo, and the sailors for slaves or ransom if high tribute could not be paid. They became known as the "Barbary Pirates" and by the late eighteenth century were dreaded not only by European maritime interests but also by those in America, as the young nation forged its own merchant marine independent of Britain. Some of the most feared were the Algerines. In 1804–5, the American navy conducted a successful war against the *pasha* of Tripoli and all but ended paying tribute to him. In the ensuing years, tribute payments to the other *pashas* ended as well. Philip Curtin et al., *African History* (New York: Longman, 1978), 180–202, 332–50.

102. Walker here refers to Pharaoh Ramses II, who questioned the existence of Moses' God. See Exodus 5:2.

103. Walker here refers to Revelation 22:13, where the angel addressing John utters, "I am the Alpha and the Omega, the first and the last, the beginning and the end."

104. Since the sixth millennium B.C., the Babylonians had inhabited the region of southern Iraq stretching from modern Baghdad to the Persian Gulf. Centered around the city of Babylon, which was renowned for its architecture and scholarship, the kingdom reached its greatest heights under Nebuchadnezzar II in the first half of the sixth century B.C. *Oxford Classical Dictionary*, 228–29.

105. The Ninevites inhabited the city of Nineveh, the ancient capital of the Assyrians located on the Tigris River a few hundred miles north of Babylon. Famed for its library and beautiful gardens, Nineveh and Assyria were at their zenith at the time of Sennacherib in the seventh century B.C. *Oxford Classical Dictionary*, 1045; *Harper Collins Bible Dictionary*, 759–60.

106. The Persians occupied roughly the land of modern Iran, where

they had lived since about 1000 B.C. The Persian Empire arose in the mid-sixth century after the military victories of Cyrus the Great, and lasted until the assaults of Alexander the Great in about 330 B.C. *Oxford Classical Dictionary*, 1144; *Harper Collins Bible Dictionary*, 832.

107. The Macedonians came from the northeastern region of the Greek peninsula and just to the west of the Balkans. Assailed by a number of neighboring powers into the fourth century B.C., Macedonia became a great independent power by the mid-fourth century, under Philip II and his son Alexander the Great. By the mid-second century B.C., however, it had become a province of Rome's empire. *Oxford Classical Dictionary*, 904–5; *Harper Collins Bible Dictionary*, 639–40.

108. The Book of Common Prayer and John Wesley's Collection of Psalms and Hymns were fundamental works for liturgy and personal devotion in early-nineteenth-century Methodist worship. The particular passages Walker quotes here were not found in any of the material reviewed.

INDEX

This index distinguishes between four parts of this volume. The Roman numeral page references refer to the introductory material in the front of the book. The boldface page references are for the original text of Walker's pamphlet. Italicized page references are for the documents relating to the pamphlet, found in the Appendix. Page numbers with note references refer to the Editor's Notes at the end of the book.